MIDDLE SCHOOL SURVIVAL GUIDE

How to Navigate Friendships, Tackle Peer Pressure, Ace Your Studies, Stay Safe Online, Understand Money Basics, Prepare for the Future, and Much More!

JAMIE THORNE

ISBN: 978-1-962481-03-8

Copyright 2023.

Elk Point Press.

For questions,

please reach out to connect@elkpointpress.com

FREE BONUS

SCAN TO GET OUR NEXT BOOK FOR FREE!

Table of Contents

INTRODUCTION: WELCOME TO MIDDLE SCHOOL!

Middle school is — in theory — cool and fun, and you will end up treasuring the years you spend here. If we're being totally real, though, you probably won't always think it's so "cool and fun" while you're there.

We don't even need to tell you that it's a crazy time to be alive. It's a crazy world out there. And, well . . . middle school can be just as *crazy*. You're certainly no longer that kid your mom and dad held in their arms or pushed around in a stroller (sorry . . . here's a spare barf bag). However, though you really want to be a fully grown, super awesome college student, you're still at least a few years away from all that. So, here you are in that strange land, stuck somewhere between kid and adult: *middle school.*

As is the case in any epic adventure, although the land is a strange one, the journey is one you'll never forget. In middle school, those friendships you formed and alliances you forged in elementary school begin to branch out even further. In elementary school, you had less freedom; you may not even have had team sports or cheerleading or anything of the sort. Now, in middle school, there's *so many options*. There are new people to meet, brand new things to do, and brand-new talents you just might discover you've had all along.

WHAT TO EXPECT
IN MIDDLE SCHOOL

People of all ages can feel a bit uncertain or uneasy about doing something new; they just might not let it show! So, give yourself some credit. You're about to dive into a brand-new world, somewhere you've never been before, a completely new experience.

A different building: The first and most obvious new thing—it's a brand-new building. Throughout the six or seven years you spent at your elementary school, you got to know your school like the back of your hand. But this middle school building . . . it's all new to you! And not only is it a new building, but it is also probably a *bigger* building. Maybe at your elementary school, it was only a 30 second walk down to the gym. Well . . . in your middle school, who knows, your gym could be a 3-minute trek away!

Many strange faces: Throughout the years, you're sure to have gotten close to a lot of people. Many of your friends, you've known since the very beginning, from the moment you walked into the very first day of elementary school. Though you've probably made some new friends and lost track with others along the way, things are certain to be much different in middle school. There will be loads of new faces, both your classmates and teachers!

Teacher per subject: Speaking of teachers—well . . . there's some changes here too! In most elementary schools, teachers teach multiple subjects, but in most middle schools, teachers stick to their favorite subject. Though this is a pretty big shift, most kids actually end up enjoying this change (if your teacher is wretched, you'll only be with them for one hour instead of three!)

The uncomfortable "P word": As you get into middle school, you may or may not have started experiencing changes in your body which point to your development into adulthood (yeah . . . *yikes!*)

Better to read about it here than hear it from your dad, right? So, it's been said, this is the beginning of your "developing years" and it's a "time of discovery." But both of those terms sound a little, uh . . . creepy, don't they? At any rate, the infamous "p word" (okay, we'll say it: puberty) comes for everybody unfortunately. It's certainly a major change we all deal with right around the middle school years. Yippee!

Bigger classes: We've mentioned that your middle school will probably be a bigger building than your elementary school was, and with that bigger building comes bigger *classes*. In elementary school your classes were probably fairly small, and you didn't have anything like chemistry labs or theater buildings that take up massive space. Though in elementary school you might have had a computer room or tech building, the one(s) in middle school are almost guaranteed to be larger.

Cafeteria culture: This is another hot topic for those fresh out of elementary. Depending on your former school, you may have become used to eating your lunch right in the class, or you may have had a small cafeteria where you gathered around with members of your class for meals. The cafeteria in middle school is *way* bigger in middle school; no longer will you be cooped up with everybody in your classroom. In middle school you'll get your pick of many more places to eat—and friends to eat with—than ever before.

Lockers: You will usually have your own locker in school, which is yours and yours alone. Middle school teaches you responsibility right from the get-go by assigning your lockers (at least that's what your teachers and parents have recommended we tell you!) The coolest thing about this is that it might be the very first place where things can be truly and only yours. In elementary school, your classmates or teachers could always go rummaging through your stuff, potentially embarrassing you, and certainly annoying you. Now, you've got at least one place where you can proudly place a sign, "Property of Me."

Gymnasiums: Gymnasiums, or "gyms," are typical parts of middle and high school. And although you probably had some kind of gym in elementary school, it was likely small and didn't have many seats. In middle school, things change. Most middle school gyms are quite large and have plenty of seating (and some pretty cool designs and logos on the floor to go with it all.)

A whole new ride to school: Ok, we admit . . . this one is pretty obvious, but it's also pretty cool. If you lived in the same house all throughout elementary school, you likely took the same route to school every day. Now, you get to shake things up a little bit, and there's sure to be many new faces — and potential friends — along the new ride.

Elective classes: When you're in middle school, you will get your first taste of things called "electives." Electives are classes you decide to take in addition to your core classes (like math, science, English, and so on.) Elective courses include things like foreign languages, theater, band, and chorus, which means you have a whole lot more say in how your day is filled.

Homework: Welp . . . so far, we've heard a lot of good news. To be totally fair, we've got to toss in a little not-so-good news. This is one of the rare cases where what your parents and teachers have told you is right on the money — there's going to be more homework than you're used to. It won't be a total academic bootcamp, but it'll definitely be an interesting change.

Extracurriculars: We've already talked about elective courses, but there are also things called "extracurricular courses." Extracurricular courses are activities take place outside of regular school hours. So, while not every elective course is an extracurricular one (take art or Spanish, for instance), many of them are (like football, theater, or band).

OVERCOMING FEAR AND ANXIETY

To handle things like fear and anxiety, it's always best to know *what* exactly they are. Let's do a little digging and find out what these terms mean.

What is fear? Fear can be so intense! It can make us react in absurd ways, often in ways that end up being quite funny in hindsight (but usually anything but funny in the moment!) It's quite normal to "freeze up" when you're faced with an intensely fearful situation. The danger (or, oftentimes, the *perceived* danger) strikes, and you can end up feeling quite crazy and out of control, out of tune with your usual self. Sometimes fear can translate into physical symptoms. If your hands and feet feel weird, you can't breathe right, your chest hurts, you're tired, dizzy, or you feel like you'll pass out, chances are fear has paid you a not so welcome visit!

And anxiety? Anxiety is when your body and mind freak out because they believe that something unpleasant will happen in the future. There's not a single soul on the planet who hasn't felt anxiety at one point or another, whether it's anxiety over going to the doctor, or perhaps anxiety over meeting new people. While fear is an emotion which is focused on the present moment, anxiety involves projection into the future, asking yourself *"what if?"* Some people are more prone to this sort of thinking than others, but it's all but impossible to escape anxiety altogether.

Dealing with Both:

Although anxiety and fear are technically two different emotions, they often crop up together (lovely, isn't it!) On a more positive note, the ways of dealing and coping with these emotions are also quite similar.

Let's take a look at a few tried and tested methods for making sure anxiety and fear can't crash your party.

Accept that you're afraid: Although it's a huge temptation to ignore or block out your feelings of fear, you can only change something when you accept it. Understanding that these feelings are common and not anything to be embarrassed about can help a ton. Simply recognizing and accepting that you're anxious can actually help you begin to feel better! If you try to take fear head-on and fight it into submission, it will only grow even stronger.

What's causing your fear: The next step is to figure out *what* you're scared of; if you're scared of middle school, chances are there's actually something more specific at the root of that fear. Maybe you're fearful of bullies, more teachers than you're used to, or the fact that your friends are going to other schools.

There's no reason to be ashamed: Be happy that you've found the cause of your fear. Fear is one of the oldest and most universal human emotions.

Replace what you are afraid of: By considering the many possible positive outcomes of a scary situation, you can replace negative emotions — like worry and doubt — with more positive ones like expectation and excitement. It might sound a little silly, but there's a good chance you might be able to replace the thought, "I'm gonna totally embarrass myself!" with the thought, "Not everybody will like me, but I'm gonna find a solid group of people who do."

Know **you're not the only one:** Whether or not they'll admit it (which they probably won't unless you're their close friend), others are scared too. The whole middle school thing is pretty intimidating; that is, unless you're some kind of superhero — in which case, you've got bigger fish to fry!

Create a working strategy to replace fear: When in doubt, you can never go wrong with making a foolproof plan! Don't be too ambitious or hard on yourself with your plan, however. Saying, "I'm going to make fifteen friends and get voted in for class president before the polls even open!" might give you a little more trouble than going with "I'm going to make a friend or two, just be myself, and even if it takes a while, I'll be just fine!"

You must be kind to yourself: Before all else, try to cut yourself a little slack. With everybody constantly telling you that you need to be nice to others, being kind to yourself can get lost in the mix. But, if you remember to show yourself a little love, then you'll be well on your way to treating others better as well. Remember—they're probably all a little scared, too!

Some tips to help overcome the "double threat":

- Take a break to do something you enjoy.
- Get some rest.
- Decide to join a group in school.
- Figure out what makes you anxious but try not to judge yourself.
- When stress or anxiety arise, speak to your parents (they might surprise you with some good advice!)
- Give your best, but don't torture yourself.
- Do some light daily exercise.
- Realize that not everything is your problem or fault—in fact, most things aren't!
- Laugh and try not to take everything super seriously.
- Try to stay a little positive, even when it feels like the world is crumbling around you.

THE IMPORTANCE OF A POSITIVE ATTITUDE

Focusing on what you can control: We have some power over certain things and none over others. For example, you're in charge of what shirt you pick out for the day, but you're not in charge of what shirt your parents decide to wear. In any case, unless your parents are total oddballs and wear weirdly offensive shirts in public that say, "My child is a doofus!" then it shouldn't really matter that you can't control what they wear anyways!

Now, obviously there are issues a lot bigger than your parents' wardrobe to worry about, things like getting bullied by your peers or called out by your teacher. However, even in these cases, the same rule still applies—you'll be a lot less stressed if you concentrate on the things, you have power over. Nobody has the power to command another person to be their friend or to make their teachers adore them (wouldn't that be freakin' awesome?) but everybody *does* have the power to focus on those things that they *can* control, from choosing an epic ensemble in the morning to having an exceptionally awesome time on a field trip.

Focusing on the good: No matter what's going on, there's *always* something good to think about. When things don't go how you want, it can be easy to keep thinking about what went wrong and what could have been. However, if you try hard to think about the good things, you can avoid these negative thoughts and stay upbeat. Finding the good in every situation will help you keep a more positive outlook, even if it isn't always easy.

Controlling your frustrations: When you're mad or upset, it can be easy to take it out on the people around you, but this usually makes the situation worse. It hurts our relationships and often makes us feel even worse, feeding into anger and frustration. While it's not good to shove your feelings in a corner and ignore them, we need to find positive ways to express ourselves. It's essential to get rid of your anger, but yelling or berating someone else is not the way to do it; it hurts your relationships and makes you look bad, and it doesn't even work, anyway! Instead of yelling at someone—or even worse, hurting them physically—try singing along to your favorite songs full blast, or use that negative energy to fuel your physical exercise by going for a run or shooting hoops.

Maintaining a sense of humor: Positivity allows you to see the funny side of things. You don't have to be hilarious; just make an effort to move on when things don't go as planned or you feel overwhelmed. Find the funny side of things and laugh it off. Other students will draw close to you if you try to keep things light-hearted.

Congratulating others: Being a good team player is appreciating the accomplishments of others, expressing congratulations and encouragement, and being genuinely happy for *everyone* on the team when someone experiences a win. You gain a realness that allows you to speak the truth when you say you're glad for them. No matter how minor the victory, you should never minimize someone else's success or accomplishments because they've worked hard and put in real effort.

Being pumped for new challenges: Every new obstacle presents an opportunity to develop and learn. Stagnation is the enemy of success; thus, it's critical to seek out ways to advance constantly. No matter how positive or negative an experience is, you can learn something from it. If you have an optimistic outlook, you'll be more enthusiastic and eager to find a solution when you encounter problems. You can overcome any challenge with an open mind and a positive outlook.

Being kinder and more understanding: When you keep a positive mind, you can better understand other people's motivations. It's better to see things from the other person's perspective instead of making a snap judgment that could hurt them. A positive attitude helps you see the good in others and keeps you from assuming the worst before you even understand the situation.

Accepting feedback: It's not easy to take criticism well, but it's the best way to improve. By receiving input on how we did, both from ourselves and others, we learn more about our strengths and where we have room to improve. A person with a development mindset believes that they always have more to learn. Those with this mindset always look for ways to improve at work, at school, and as people in general. So, don't be afraid of less-than-stellar feedback; instead, look at it with an open mind and use the help it gives you.

EMBRACING CHANGES AND CHALLENGES

Everyone needs to learn to embrace changes and challenges; things will not remain the same forever. Even your body is a testament to that cycle of change. So, see change and challenges as part of your life, things that make life more interesting. Adolescents (a fancy word for people who are in the process of changing from kids to adults) face many difficulties and changes. You're still developing your sense of self and understanding how that affects your relationships and opportunities.

Here, we've listed a few ways that you can adjust to change, meet challenges in a positive and productive manner, and learn to embrace the curveballs that life throws your way.

Reduce expectations: You may have had lofty hopes for middle school. In your thought process, you may have believed it was a place where it's *all* good or all bad. You will come to realize, though, that nothing is permanent. No doubt you learned that lesson already, when you discovered that some of your elementary friends were going off to another school. Though there's nothing wrong with hoping for a particular outcome, you should prepare yourself to keep going if things turn out differently.

Accepting whatever comes from your new school is easier if you have few expectations. Because you aren't spending all your time coming up with lists of things you want, you can better prepare to deal with whatever challenges life throws your way. So, don't expect too much, set small expectations, and you'll be even happier when good things do come your way.

Accept new things: The only constant in life is that life is constantly changing. As time passes, you will learn that new situations can arise quickly and without warning. Knowing this as a kid will help you a lot, but more importantly, you must learn to embrace change as part of life. Instead of denying and fighting change, recognize it and let it happen when it comes.

Know that you are getting better: When you accept change, welcome it, and learn from it, you will always get better. Being able to accept change over and over again makes you strong. Strength comes from inside; we are strengthened when we stay standing while everything else falls apart, even when howling storms surround us.

Learn from new experiences: You'll see growth possibilities all around if you're willing to adjust to new situations. At first, you may not know the importance of life's big changes; however, when you examine and accept the changes, you'll learn something that will change your life. Change can be your best teacher—but only if you allow yourself to learn from it.

Take in the advice: Your personal development will be influenced by how much you allow external matters to affect your life. Your life will become much more peaceful as a result of accepting change. You'll learn that life's unexpected challenges can't destroy you if you don't let them! Accepting change will allow your understanding of life to mature right alongside your body. It's not always easy, though; not even every adult has gotten there yet. Take life's lessons; learning to accept them as they come is the journey of a lifetime, so why not get a jumpstart now?

CHAPTER ONE: MAKING AND KEEPING FRIENDS

Imagine being at the same school for years and years but never making any friends there ... Sounds pretty terrible, doesn't it? Though school can downright suck sometimes, it's always just a little bit easier with some trusted pals by your side throughout it all.

You have the potential to acquire a wide variety of abilities — including the ability to make and keep friends. Not only will learning how to approach people, carry on conversations with them, and keep relationships going make you a happier person at school, but these are skills that you'll be grateful to have learned for the rest of your life.

Middle School and Friendship

Having genuine friends is of the utmost importance, for the sake of your health (mental, educational, social, and emotional) as well as your overall growth as a person. It can even affect your academic performance, as it will improve as a direct result of the increase in both your self-esteem and self-confidence that it provides. Look, we understand you're probably rolling your eyes at this, but it's the honest truth. We swear!

Middle school is an amazing time in one's life, but if you aren't having fun, what's the point?

THE ART OF
MAKING FRIENDS

Just be yourself: Yes, it's a little corny to say, but if you want to have real, long-lasting friendships, one of the most important things you can do is *just be yourself.* Don't try to be someone you're not just to fit in with a particular group. In any case, keeping up the act would eventually become a total nightmare! Real friends will like you for who you are, and if you're honest, you'll have a better chance of developing friendships that will last a lifetime.

Be open and friendly: If you want to make friends, you have to put yourself out there. If you want people to approach you, use welcoming body language. Keep your head up, shoulders back, and eyes forward as you greet others. It's okay to go up to a stranger and introduce yourself. A simple "hello" could open doors you never imagined possible. Keep your arms near your sides and open up (avoid crossing your arms across your chest.) People will feel more comfortable talking to you if they perceive you as approachable and friendly. Give people a pleasant nod and a smile as you go by them or make casual eye contact with them in the cafeteria.

Make conversation: There are countless opportunities to meet new people and deepen existing relationships at school. You can ask the student next to you in class about how they handled the most recent assignment. Asking someone a question that focuses on them is a brilliant way to start a discussion, because most people enjoy chatting about themselves. Let them talk about themselves for a change! Ask someone you're hanging out with about their favorite subjects, extracurricular activities, or television series. Don't leapfrog from one issue to another. Instead, you should pose a question and engage the other person in conversation about that. When the discussion stalls, shift gears. If you're timid, approaching strangers to initiate a conversation can feel like a massive leap of faith. However, it will get easier with practice. If you're ever feeling down about being shy, just remember, many of the world's most powerful and incredible people were once (or are still) a little shy!

Practice active listening: It shows when you take the time to actually listen to someone. Show genuine curiosity and attention when conversing with others. This is the first and most important step in forming a friendship with them.

Put yourself in extracurriculars: Getting involved in clubs and other extracurricular activities is a terrific way to broaden your social circle by meeting classmates who share your interests. There's sure to be a group or organization that suits your interests, whether in sports, the arts, or something else entirely.

- If you see an opportunity to find students who share your interests, but there's not a group for that interest already, form your own club! At your first club gathering, have everyone introduce and tell a bit about themself.
- If you don't feel comfortable forming one, an easier option is to just join a club about something that you're curious about.
- Choose a sport you're interested in and find out how to join. You and your teammates can become close friends over time.

Go to social gatherings: The best place to make new friends is at social gatherings. It's perfectly acceptable to attend most of these gatherings alone; try to chat with at least a few people once you get there. If going alone makes you uncomfortable, ask a friend or classmate you'd like to get to know better to join you. That way, you'll always have someone to talk to, no matter what happens.

Take an active role in class: Classroom discussions are not only a great chance to ask questions and get answers from your professor, they're also a great way to meet new people. Participating in class discussions lets your peers know that you share their enthusiasm for the subject. This can lead to friendships and enjoyable chats outside of the classroom.

Eat in the cafeteria: Seek out tables with empty seats; always eat with others. If you're anxious, choose a table with only one or two other students. Go over, politely request a chair, and jump right into the conversation. It's natural to feel apprehensive around new people at first. If you had a good time at lunch, ask the folks you sat with if they'd like to sit together the following day.

Jump out of your comfort zone: If you feel uncertain about yourself, you might be tempted to decline social invitations. However, resist the temptation; social interaction is vital to expanding your social circle. Try it out; you might actually enjoy it more than you think!

Enroll in electives of interest to you: Ask your homeroom teacher or guidance counselor about available electives and add the ones that pique your interest to your schedule. You'll have a jump start, because you'll already have the same interest as the other students in the class!

MAINTAINING FRIENDSHIPS: THE DOS AND DON'TS

Our friends can actually get tired of our annoying habits or other quirks, especially if they have patiently put up with these for a long time and have talked to us many times about changing. It could also be that we are too negative, selfish, careless, or don't respect their boundaries. As you start middle school, you must learn the skills you need to keep the friends you have and also find out the bad habits you need to avoid.

How to Maintain Friendships

Forgive them: It's important to remember that everyone makes mistakes, but also that friends can easily forgive each other. To make it easy to forgive, imagine yourself as the offender. Would you want to be forgiven?

Keep your promises: Yes, you're young, and it seems like a grown-up thing to tell you to keep your promises. However, remember, adults who don't trust others were once young like you. Maybe they once had someone they believed in, but that person kept failing them.

Show kindness: You should try to be kind to everyone you meet. Kindness draws people to you; people want to be friends with a kind person, even when they are not kind.

Be their cheer captain: Praise your friends and compliment or commend them when they do something well or are trying their best. They would love you being there for them. Be genuine, and people will be able to tell you actively care about them.

Talk before reacting: If a problem or issue is unclear to you, you should discuss it with your friends before reacting negatively to it. If your friend forgets to return something they borrowed from you, ask why they haven't returned before responding angrily, and let them explain themselves.

Be respectful: Whether you are just chatting or cracking a joke, do so in a polite manner. You don't want your friend to feel humiliated because you said something cruel or demeaning about them, even as a joke.

Things you shouldn't do.

Don't lie to them: You should never lie to anyone. Don't make up stories or try to cover up the truth; always tell it like it is, especially to people who care about you. It hurts people when you don't trust them enough to speak the truth.

Don't gossip about them: Talking bad about your friends, especially when they're not there to defend themselves, is just wrong. It means you are not really their friend, plain and simple, and you've just been pretending.

Don't criticize them: Your friends have their own lives, and they have their faults. Don't attack them when they do something you think isn't good enough. If you're really their friend, you need to show them a little grace.

Don't disregard their ideas: When there's a problem to be solved, listen when your friends give you their honest opinion. If you decide not to go with their ideas, make sure to tell them why.

Don't be arrogant: This is the most effective method for ending friendships. Even if you're doing better than they are, do your best to be humble. If you do better than them in schoolwork, don't call them "dumb." Besides, they're probably better than you at some other things!

Don't be too busy for them: Making and keeping friends is an investment of time and energy, but it's possible to do so despite a busy schedule. Why not do some of those activities together? Find ways to include your friends, even when your schedules conflict.

HANDLING CONFLICTS WITH FRIENDS

We know that your friends will be young people from different families, with different cultures, religions, and experiences. So, they may do things you are not happy or familiar with, but they may not even understand if they have offended you. Many shallow friendships end after a fight because there isn't enough depth to make it worth the trouble to make up. Even when a friendship gets stronger, it's still possible for conflicts to happen, which can seriously strain or even end a relationship.

What to Do When There is Conflict:

- Don't react immediately.

- Take a moment to think about why you are bothered.
- Ask yourself, "Did they do it on purpose?"
- Plan your words before speaking.
- Whatever answer you get, let them know immediately why you're bothered.
- Don't personally attack them.
- Don't accuse them of trying to hurt or annoy you, even if you feel that way.
- Try not to speak with anger. Explain why whatever has happened bothered you.
- Be understanding; your friend will sometimes see a situation differently than you do.
- A true friend will apologize.
- Whether they do it then or later, accept their apology.
- Let it go. Don't hold a grudge!

THE IMPORTANCE OF QUALITY OVER QUANTITY

Most middle schoolers—and everybody else—have learned as they grow older that having many friends is a waste of time if they don't care about your personal life. The truth is, you don't need a whole lot of friends, just the few that will stand up for you when you can't stand up for yourself. Take this situation for example:

It's crucial that you don't look at friendship just in terms of quantity, because many people may actually like you, due to your ability to relate to them. However, they may be relating to you conditionally; when those conditions are not met, they will leave you. True friends of quality are there for you whether you deliver on those conditions or not.

CHAPTER TWO: STANDING UP TO PEER PRESSURE

It's said that people are "social creatures." Even those of us who are particularly introverted or "lone wolf"-type characters will still (however begrudgingly) admit that it's always nice to have a little social support. However, there's social *support* in the form of friends, and then there's social *pressure* in the form of feeling pressured to behave or think in a certain way to please others. While your best friends would never try to change you, others around you just may try to get a little "something extra" out of you.

This is what people call "peer pressure." Peer pressure is an extremely common thing, but there are times when things can get a little out of hand.

UNDERSTANDING PEER PRESSURE

There are different types of peer pressure; it can be good or bad.

Good peer pressure: This is when someone tells you to do something good, like be kind to others, work hard in school, help at home, and stay away from alcohol and drugs. Your friends can help you make good decisions and do the right thing. So, hanging out with people who make you a better person is essential. But be aware . . . good peer pressure is sometimes rare!

Bad peer pressure: Bad peer pressure is when one of your friends tries to push you to do something bad for you. This could mean skipping school, lying, stealing, cheating, drinking, or even doing drugs. It's possible you'll feel pressured into doing something against your better judgment. It can be easy to fall for this kind of pressure if you're trying to gain popularity and social acceptance.

SAYING NO: STRATEGIES AND TECHNIQUES

It's possible to develop your natural personality to where you can calmly and confidently look peer pressure in the eye and tell it to, as you may have heard your dad say from time to time, "pound sand." Believe it or not, adults deal with the exact same thing, except the people around them are a lot sneakier about it. The difference between the kids at lunch daring you to pull down your pants and your dad's boss telling him to stay late and miss your choir concert can be a smaller one than you'd think!

Some ways to say "no."

- You must first know that you *can* say "no." People may want you to do something, but you can say, "No, I'm good." It's your right to say no, and you may be surprised to find that some people will actually respect you for it.
- "Well . . . I appreciate the invitation, but that's not gonna happen." Even if you don't "appreciate" it, sometimes it can be disarmingly witty to say something to this effect. If you can essentially tell them to "get the heck out of here" with a smile, then you'll have done your job!

- It's perfectly fine to say "no" without giving a reason. Nobody is entitled to your reasoning or rationale (even though your parents sure make it seem like they are!)
- After somebody asks you to do something stupid, look into their eyes with concern and ask, "Are you ok?" This one is actually backed by science! Asking if someone is ok can disarm them and can make them a little self-conscious and begin to ask themself, "Wait . . . *am* I ok? Did I just embarrass . . . *myself*?!" This usually ends in the infamous "mic drop."
- Say "no" by asking them to do *you* a favor. No . . . this one isn't nearly as stupid as it sounds either; it's actually fiendishly clever! If someone asks you to do something embarrassing or just plain stupid, you can always tell them, "Well . . . I won't be able to do that for you unfortunately, but I did have something I'd like your help with . . ." You can take a little pause for dramatic effect. And after they finally go, "Yeah . . .?" you can feel free to make up some incredibly outlandish thing you need their help with. "So . . . I've got this older friend in the Marines, right? He's like 6'6" and 300 pounds of raw muscle. He's always telling me that the first person to do a hundred shirtless pushups on the cafeteria table gets dibs on everything for the rest of the year. Apparently, this is common sense to everybody . . . or it *should* be at least. Anyways, I seriously doubt you'd have what it takes to pull something like that off . . ." After this, feel free to walk away and never return!

Peer Pressure and Online Behavior

The way people relate to each other has changed because of how quickly social media has become accepted. It's easy to always be linked to the internet; people can stay inside and keep in touch with all their friends through social media sites like Snapchat, TikTok, WhatsApp, Facebook, and Instagram.

You're now more connected than ever to many more people your age. Being accepted by peers is a very important part of growing up as a young person. Social media is a platform that brings more "friends" to you, increasing peer pressure, which can sometimes seem very serious. This is especially true when metrics like shares, number of likes, and comments are used to measure popularity and how much people like someone.

Some Online Behaviors That Are a Result of Peer Pressure:

Cyberstalking: Because cyberstalking frequently involves a real threat to the victim's safety, it is considered more destructive than other forms of cyberbullying. Cyberstalking is a state of online harassment in which the perpetrator persistently contacts the victim via electronic means. Cyberstalkers are people that harass or threaten their target repeatedly through electronic messages. They may explicitly encourage others to do the same, or they may pose as the victim to solicit contact from others.

Catfishing: When someone attempts to conceal their true identity, they're "catfishing." Catfishing occurs when an imposter uses other people's personal information and images to build a fake social media profile, presenting themselves as those people.

Trolling: Internet trolls deliberately try to annoy or insult others to get a reaction. Although some trolls participate in cyberbullying, others may use comparatively harmless pranks. Trolls and cyberbullies may not always share the same objectives, but they use similar means and aim for the same results: harassing someone to get a reaction.

Cyberbullying: When discussing harassment among young people or at school, the term "cyberbullying" is often used. With a few key exceptions, cyberbullying is frequently compared to traditional forms of bullying. It's not uncommon for victims of cyberbullying to be in the dark about *who* is harassing them and *why*. Cyberbullying can be as easy as publishing false rumors about someone online to incite hate or encouraging others to engage in online smearing of a target, either directly or indirectly.

Examples of Cyberbullying:

Outing: A person gets "outed" when embarrassing and/or private information is released online without their consent. Outings might reveal serious or humiliating things a person does when they think no one is watching.

Fraping: People "frape" others using their login details to access their social media accounts and post inappropriate content in their name. Fraping is considered a form of hacking and can result in serious consequences if the victim decides to press charges.

Ghost accounts: People may build phony profiles to cyberbully others anonymously. The cyberbully may even use the victim's email or phone. It would appear that someone else sent the threats. Cyberbullies create fake personas to avoid exposure.

Note: Online impersonation and lies about a person can cause unalterable damage to their reputation. You can never be sure you've deleted unpleasant remarks or other stuff from the internet.

TURNING NEGATIVE PEER PRESSURE INTO POSITIVE INFLUENCE

Peer pressure is one of the best ways to model appropriate behavior and make wise decisions. If you have friends who are respectful, intellectual, and responsible, you'll start to realize that you're absorbing those qualities too.

Negative peer pressure often occurs, but as you begin middle school, knowing what you stand for is the only way to turn you friends around with positive influence. Trust your gut when figuring out what's right and wrong. Think about the situation. You probably already know what to do. Knowing what to do will make you more determined. Ask an adult for help. They can help you come out unscathed and even better from negative peer pressure.

CHAPTER THREE:
THE WORLD
OF ACADEMICS

The middle school years are when you can set yourself up for future success in high school and whatever will be your chosen field (yeah . . . or at least this is the dry way that your parents have phrased it, right?). Well, even though your parents may not have been exactly entertaining with their delivery, they've got a point. The hard work you put in in middle school can have some pretty solid results down the road, in High School and beyond. And at any rate, the study habits you form in middle school will help guide you throughout the rest of your school years.

To say it again as your parents would say it to really hammer the point home: Doing well in middle school will help put you on the appropriate route toward academic and professional success. *Boring*? Yes. But it's *no joke*!

In Middle School, You Will:

- be taught how to generate original ideas that are both active and engaging from your everyday experiences.
- learn to give feedback that is both high-quality and timely on the subjects you are taught.
- participate in activities that are more advanced than what you did in elementary school. Some of these exercises will require you to think critically, give solutions, and provide your reasoning process. You will have lessons, presentations, exercises, and examinations combining both systems you used in elementary school and new approaches.
- be encouraged by teachers to learn by yourself and in groups.
- have a lot of opportunities to work on your presentation skills and become better at exams.

EFFECTIVE
STUDY HABITS

Know you are good enough: Understand that you are good enough. Everything you need to do well in academics is in you already. Since you're young, your brain is still developing, and you have very few responsibilities to distract you from school. Your parents or guardians will (hopefully) do all the mature stuff in order to help you focus.

A place to study: Find a good place to study, then head there. Having a quiet, peaceful place to study is one of the most crucial elements to doing well in school. The area you are looking for is a place where loud sounds or people who are always trying to get your attention won't bother you. You can start in a quiet part of your house, a public library, or even a coffee shop.

Set goals: Establish objectives for every study session. Make sure that, as you sit to study, you have specific goals in mind. These can be based on specific classes, or particular pieces of content. You could aim to learn a part of the subject for one hour and 30 minutes. If you don't achieve the goal, though, it's okay. It's normal for studying to take more time than anticipated sometimes. Continue and set up another study session.

Schedule breaks: Taking regular breaks can improve memory recall, help maintain focus, and give a needed boost to your energy levels. During the break, you can take a walk, check your phone, eat something, enjoy more energetic tunes, and stretch or rest. Ensure these activities during the break are brief; your breaks should be 10 to 25 minutes every 50 to 90 minutes; it may take a while to find the ideal break schedule for you. If you're working at a computer, make sure you give your eyes a break by focusing on something far away for a few minutes twice an hour or so.

Your phone is an enemy: You must already know that we can be easily distracted by our phones. Turning off your notifications, putting your phone on "do not disturb," or putting your phone in a bag where it can't be seen are all strategies that assist you in maintaining your focus.

Perform test-taking practices: Tests and practice exams have long been used by students as valuable ways to learn and remember information. Taking a test forces, us to remember facts, which research shows is a powerful and effective way to retain what we've learned.

Summarize what you've learned: Another good way to retain information is to put it into your own words. You can summarize what you just read by rephrasing the key concepts into your own words. Pretend you are explaining the subject to another person; it may surprise you to know that teaching someone else is one of the best ways to learn!

Let people help you: Seek assistance from a friend, the best student in your class, your teacher, and anyone else who can help. We all struggle with a problem or subject from time to time, and a different view on the issue can be offered by someone who can lead you through it.

Go online: As you study and cross-check things online, there are a lot of resources you can use, including videos on topics you're studying. Just make sure you verify your sources, and always fact-check the information you find online!

A study group or friend: You can decide whether you work best with a group or just a buddy, depending on how each affects your concentration. If you and your guys are on the same page regarding the importance of studying and will help prevent each other from becoming distracted, then go for it. Keeping yourself accountable and focused is helpful if you study with a friend or two, even if you're working on a different subject.

Music: As you concentrate on your studies, you could play some music that is soothing and instrumental. There are certain advantages to studying while listening to music, including improving your mood and reducing stress. However, avoid fast beats, overly noisy music, or music containing lyrics; those kinds of music don't help your focus, and may actually distract you.

Give yourself a treat: Rewarding yourself with something you enjoy can be fantastic motivation to reach your objective. After a long day of studying or after finishing a test or exam, treat yourself to your favorite food, engage in an activity you enjoy doing, play games, watch your favorite TV show, or relax with friends.

Maintain a healthy sleep schedule: better sleep can boost your mood and improve your relationships with others. Sleep deprivation has been linked to decreased cognitive function, including a shorter attention span and poor performance during tests and exams.

Eat the right food: Science believes that eating foods like fruits, vegetables, nuts, unsaturated oils and plant-based proteins helps the brain perform better, so try to eat more of these healthy foods.

Avoid eating too much processed sugar and other empty calories whenever possible.

COPING WITH ACADEMIC STRESS

The worst thing you can do to get through a stressful time is to ignore it, leaving it to build up. If you do nothing to fix a problem, it usually just gets worse. Developing strength, taking control, surrounding yourself with people who support you, and keeping a positive outlook are all wonderful ways to deal with academic stress.

Dealing with Stress

Be true to yourself: Recognize when you're having difficulty in your academic classes and take action to address the problem. Rather than putting off the work until it becomes too much to handle, acknowledge that you're having trouble and then get to work solving the problem. If you have difficulty overcoming your challenges, ask your parent, a friend, or a teacher for assistance.

Take time for yourself: Make some "me time" for yourself. Because your academic workload has increased, you'll need more time to engage in activities you enjoy. It's essential to schedule time for relaxing activities such as resting, reading for pleasure, playing games, and even chatting with your friends. You can have this time between classes, or during breaks or rest periods in school.

Prioritize: Setting priorities means working smarter. Assign importance for each academic subject and focus on the ones that will take the most effort from you to deal with first; then save the ones that are the easiest to deal with last. Recognize that it takes effort to complete everything you set out to do. Obtain advice from teachers on how to manage your time more effectively.

Be realistic, but optimistic: Maintain a practical perspective, giving equal weight to the benefits and disadvantages of any given situation. Keep in mind that our thoughts dictate and determine our behavior, so try to look on the bright side. Be aware of the nice things happening, and be thankful for your life, parents and friends. You could even challenge yourself to write down things you are grateful for.

Be good to your body: Maintain a healthy lifestyle by getting at least eight hours of sleep nightly. You're young, so do your best to get at least thirty minutes of daily physical activity in the fresh air and sunshine, even—or perhaps especially—during stressful study sessions; as we said earlier, physical activity, like walking or running, will improve your academic performance.

Develop close relationships with your loved ones: Your parents, friends, and teachers are people that can help you with academics. When middle school seems stressful, these people will be happy to be available for you because they care about you. So let them know what's going on, so they can help you!

TIME MANAGEMENT SKILLS

Many of your schoolmates may need more preparation for school, not to mention help learning how to manage their time. Elementary school is much less demanding than middle school, so many freedoms you enjoy will not be encouraged in your new school. Because your teachers already see you as grown, they will expect you to be responsible with your time. The process of planning, organizing and arranging how to allocate one's time to various academic and non-academic activities is referred to as "time management."

Being purposeful with how you spend your time is essential, whether you're a student or anyone else. Taking charge of the time that you have and maximizing it for productivity, concentration, and relaxation is the best way to maintain balance in your life. Time management is, therefore, an important skill to have as a student. You will need to use time well in study sessions, activities, and exams.

A guide on how to manage your time.

- Knowing how you spend your time is crucial to time management. Discover where you're losing and spending time. If you are not sure how you're spending time, how can you deal with it?
- If you've discovered things that are wasting your time, ask yourself how important those things are. Find a way to

work them into your schedule if essential. If not, cut them out!

- Make a daily schedule. Your schedule should reflect how much of your day you spend in class, the cafeteria and other places. Managing your schedule is more important than making a to-do list for student time management. A daily schedule template helps you plan, prioritize, and avoid procrastination.

- Make sure to schedule downtime, socializing, and time with your friends. Studying must be balanced with eating, exercising, socializing, and other "non-school" activities that make you happy and energized.

- Define your success, both academic and non-academic. When you define, you can pick the correct route to take; this saves you time. Most people need to set goals carefully to avoid taking the wrong road.

- Divide large tasks into manageable pieces. Goal setting requires breaking ambitious goals into bite-sized pieces. This will prevent procrastination and motivate you to work quickly.

- Some activities may take longer than you think. It's easy to overestimate your available time when planning your day. Give yourself extra wiggle room for familiar tasks, and even more slack for new or unfamiliar ones.

- Schedule breaks! Taking breaks helps you stay productive. When should you stop? When you get hungry, distracted, sleepy, or fidgety. Take a break if this happens. Having a fidget toy — like a spinner or puzzle cube — on hand can help if you start to feel antsy.

SEEKING HELP
WHEN NEEDED

Your academics include various activities, which you may have issues with because you are just starting, so your teachers are ready to help. Your confidence, grades, and future learning opportunities could be jeopardized if you don't seek help when you need it.

Know when you need help: Before anyone can help you, you have to be strong enough to admit that you need help! You are going to middle school for the first time, so it's natural to be confused sometimes. If you're worried other people might make fun of you, you can meet the teacher after class and explain to them what you need. Your teachers will be glad to help!

Seeking help is smart: It's important to note that seeking help is <u>not</u> a sign of weakness. It shows you are strong enough to speak up for what you want. It's wise to ask for help; if you get the help you need, you can then help other people. If you don't, things may never get better.

Determine your problem: Ask yourself if your problem is related to school or if it's something more personal. You need to know exactly what the problem is before asking people for help. People are good at different things, so think about who the best person would be to ask. Your parents will do whatever they can to help you with home and family-related matters. Your siblings and friends may be better people to talk to about social issues.

At the same time, your teachers and counselors are trained to help you deal with any problems that might affect how well you do in school. Though social issues can be discussed with friends, something as serious as bullying should be brought to a teacher or counselor.

Who do I ask for help? As you start middle school, your parents, teachers, siblings, and friends are the first people you'll turn to when you need to talk to someone. This is because, except for your friends, everyone mentioned is in a more senior position. This means they have more experience and have probably dealt with problems you have or will have.

These are great ways to show how much you want to improve yourself. It makes sense to first think about your allies. Then, think about other people based on what you know about their access to the resources, knowledge, or skills you need.

Plan what to say: If you have a few questions ready, it will be much easier for anyone you ask for help to understand your problem better and help you come up with ways to deal with it. You can write down the issues and turn them into questions for your counselor. Planning lets you make the most of the helper's time, shows you are ready for answers, and keeps you on track.

Think about the timing: When you need help, you can ask your parents or friends, or anyone else you want, if they have time to help you. You can tell them if it's an emergency or not and ask them for a time to meet. By making an appointment, you can be sure they will have the time and resources to help you solve your problem.

Be positive: When you ask for help, try not to say anything negative about yourself. It can be tempting to complain every now and then; this could be a way to protect yourself if you don't like asking for help. No one wants to hear you say bad things about yourself, though. If you ask in a positive way, it will help.

Be confident and speak up: People are usually glad to share what they know and will probably be flattered that you asked. If you don't ask for help, you probably won't get it, and even if you do, it might not be what you wanted. People may not understand how urgently you need help, and they can't know you need help if you don't ask for it! Don't think asking for help makes you weak, insecure, or ashamed. So, if you need something, ask for it, even if it's from a classmate. This shows that you are sure of yourself and want to learn.

Define your needs: By making your request clear, the person who can help will know what you want to get out of the conversation and what problem you are trying to solve. This kind of detail gives people a sense of the situation and a place to start working together. It also lets them know how long they have to answer. So, explain the problem and what kind of help you want.

Be thankful and honest: The person you're talking to will appreciate your acknowledgement of the fact that they're trying to help you. Even if it makes you feel bad that you needed help, please don't act like it never happened. Tell the other person that you appreciate what they did for you. Try to say this as soon as possible after getting help.

CHAPTER FOUR:
BEING ACTIVE
AND PLAYING SPORTS

Everybody needs some kind of regular physical activity, be it sports, dancing, or just leisurely walks. And, to put it as your parents probably have—quite annoyingly, no doubt—growing young bodies such as yours especially benefit from regular exercise or stretching.

Working out improves cardiovascular health, boosts energy, and increases oxygen flow to the entire body—including the brain. Exercising allows you to build muscles, grow stronger bones, and lose weight. In terms of youth and energy, there's no better time to start letting those athletic juices flow than *right now*. Remember how your grandma is always whining about her achy joints? Yeah... go ahead and live it up, because you've still got half a century to go before, you'll even have to worry about any of that!

But there is little time . . .

You're now aware that physical activity is crucial to your health, but finding time to work out every day is challenging, especially now that you're in middle school. You have lots of classwork, club activities, homework, friends—basically, there are plenty of things that take your time. So, the question is: how do you find the time to exercise?

The Solution: Sports

The solution is participating in organized sports, whether they're school and community leagues. Organized activities in schools such as track and field, physical education, and the different school teams sports are opportunities to use. There are even posters encouraging participation in these groups around the school.

The activity levels of children who participate in organized sports are consistently higher than those don't. The presence of a coach and the requirement for regular attendance at practices are certainly some of the contributing factors. Coaches are helpful because they can provide high-intensity training without risking injury and boost morale.

THE BENEFITS OF PHYSICAL ACTIVITY

What is physical activity?

Any movement that requires a release of kinetic energy (basically, movement) from the body is considered physical activity. Increasing your level of physical activity is one of the best ways to boost your health and happiness. It's important to keep moving, no matter your age, to keep your blood pumping smoothly, muscles healthy, and your bones strong. Here are some of the benefits of exercise:

Preventing weight gain: You've probably heard people say that eating junk food makes people overweight, and yes, that's true. However, lack of exercise is actually the main reason most people become overweight; it's absolutely necessary to move your body to prevent weight gain. There are many problems with being overweight, including the fact that you'll need a lot of help to do stuff. Obesity negatively affects your heart, kidney, lungs, liver, blood vessels—basically your entire body.

Maintaining a low blood pressure: This may be the first time you've heard of this, as high blood pressure is mainly discussed among adults. However, having too high of a blood pressure can cause many problems, up to and including death. Exercise lowers your chances of developing this condition.

Sound sleep: Physical activities tire your body out because you use a lot of energy. When you use up a lot of energy, your body needs to rest (shocking, we know!) You'll sleep much more soundly when you've exerted yourself, which means you'll be more energetic and alert the following day.

Preventing stiffness: You know how hinges on outdoor buildings can get rusty if you don't use them? Your joints are the same way, becoming stiffer the less you move them. A healthy amount of physical activity strengthens the muscles around your joints, which can help prevent the development of conditions like arthritis; it can even help minimize the pain that people who already suffer from arthritis!

Strengthening muscles: You may have seen people in gyms lifting and carrying heavy objects. Doing this helps them build and maintain their muscle strength. You don't have to be a bodybuilder to benefit from increased strength!

Improving cognitive function: Physical activity can improve the speed of your brain's functioning. Staying active increases blood flow to the brain, upping the levels of oxygen it receives. You also use different parts of the brain when you move your body than when you're doing things like reading or solving math problems. Part of the brain's function includes memory, so don't be surprised when your ability to remember things improves as you exercise.

Preventing sickness and disease: Physical activity does a lot to improve your overall health. Having a healthy body means you'll get sick less often, and staying active can also lower your chances of developing chronic diseases like type 2 diabetes, heart disease, and many kinds of cancer.

Longer lifespan: Another advantage of improved health is an increased lifespan. Regular physical activity keeps your body and brain healthy, meaning you're less likely to contract life-threatening illnesses. Since you'll also be avoiding conditions like cancer, arthritis, and heart disease, you'll live longer, and your quality of life will be better. Keeping all parts of the body active is crucial to health, happiness, and long life.

BALANCING ACADEMICS AND SPORTS

If you have now joined an organized sporting activity, you need to learn to balance that with school and all your other activities. The exercise helps you maintain your physical and mental health, but you have to be able to put that improved brain function to work in your academic classes, too! Let's take a look at how you can balance your academics and sports.

Know your priorities: You are not being told to choose between academics and sports; they're both important. However, sometimes you'll have to prioritize your homework. After all, in some schools, you're only allowed to represent the school in sports if you do well in class.

Talk to your helpers: We have mentioned earlier that it is not a sign of weakness to inform your parents, coaches and teachers of your plans and to seek assistance when necessary. They can't know how much is already going on in your life if you don't tell them! Because they have been in similar situations, the teachers and coaches will likely be understanding.

Form a strategy: Remember how we talked about making a schedule? Time management skills are vital to succeed in academics *and* sports. Make a plan that will help you succeed. You can get a better sense of how much time you have each day by writing down your commitments, such as practice, training, upcoming games, due dates for homework and schoolwork— factor in time for recreation, rest, travel, eating, and socializing, too. You can use a physical calendar or planner, or even a smartphone app.

Put your weekends to good use: The weekend is a time to relax and recharge. As someone committed to sports and academics, you can use this time to get ahead on your studies. It's not that you shouldn't relax on the weekend, but rather focus on getting the most out of your time.

Use free periods: Take advantage of your time during free periods like study hall to get ahead on your schoolwork, since you're already at school anyway. Make use of the school's library and other resources. You'll have some other opportunities to get some work done or study as well, including the ride to and from school or practice and during lunch.

Don't put things off: What you postpone today will still be there tomorrow, and then you'll be scrambling to figure out how to cram everything into a single sitting. Don't put things off; time is of the essence.

SPORTSMANSHIP: WINNING AND LOSING WITH GRACE

What is sportsmanship?

People may have different ideas about how to act at a sporting event. However, your attitude toward a sport, a player or a sport is what sportsmanship is all about. Good sportsmanship is displayed by things like being polite to other players, being brave, not giving up, and being honest. Your attitude should ultimately be showing regard to one's superiors and respecting one's opponents.

Why is it important?

You can apply the morals you learn in sportsmanship to other aspects of your life. The same traits present in a good sport are also seen in responsible, respected, and successful adults. Your opponents and teammates will study your demeanor and be influenced by it, so set a good example.

Sportsmanship Lessons

All about respect: At all times, you should respect your teammates, opposing players, instructors, coaches, game officials, and spectators. If you disagree with your coach, speak to them in private in a respectful manner. You have to honor and uphold the game's values above all else.

Modesty: A sportsmanlike behavior is to accept defeat as an inevitable part of competition. No taunting, embarrassing, or humiliating an opponent or game official is tolerated in sports.

Self-Control: A sportsman shows self-control when dealing with game officials, even when they disagree. You should keep calm, reflect on what went wrong, and prepare for the next encounter.

Follow the rules: Being a good sport means understanding and adhering to the established guidelines for competition. You should master your sport's fundamentals and the laws governing it.

Be accountable: Taking responsibility for your actions and upholding your values should be your top priority. Even if you have failed and are being blamed for your mistake, you must accept your part.

Avoid accusation: The sportsmanlike player doesn't use a bad situation to point fingers or make excuses. Making mistakes is inherent to being human.

Always put fun first: A good sport enjoys themselves because they care more about the playing the game than the outcome. Having a good time together is crucial to everyone's success in learning the game.

Listen: A sportsmanlike player listens to and follows the coach's instructions because they understand that everyone on the team benefits when people work together.

Teamwork: Recognizing the importance of teamwork is an essential component of being a good athlete. As a result, you should understand that whatever you do reflects on the team you're a part of.

Aim for peak performance: A good sportsperson knows how to do their job well, keeps improving, and gives it their all when competing. Your success depends on how hard you work to reach your full potential. The lessons and value of sports are not found in winning or losing, but in the competition and the noble pursuit of victory.

NON-SPORT ACTIVITIES AND HOBBIES

Playing a musical instrument: Studying music has been linked to improved memory, self-esteem, mathematical and linguistic skills, and overall intelligence. You'll be better off, but it'll take discipline, concentration, and effort. If your school has a marching band, you can even get exercise while you play!

Birdwatching: Birds are just one of nature's many stunning creations. As a hobby, birdwatching can help you connect with the natural world and gain valuable insights into sustainable living. Birdwatching is a peaceful pastime that can help one relax and develop patience. This is another hobby that doubles as an opportunity for exercise, too, since the best way to find birds is to get out in nature!

Learning a new language: Studying a new language will likely excite your brain. Learning about a new country and its people is a great mental challenge and an excellent way to broaden your worldview.

Hiking: Hiking has recreational, meditative, and physical benefits. It's also a chance to spend time with your friends by walking far distances while conversing and having fun.

Puzzles: Puzzles are a fantastic pastime because they provide a fun mental challenge. As you solve that puzzle, you get to bask in the glow of accomplishment. This activity is great for relieving boredom and improving spatial task performance, hand-eye coordination, and abstract thinking.

Bowling: Bowling is a great physical activity that helps with hand-eye coordination, balance, and strength. The mental benefits are just as noticeable as the physical ones, especially considering the need for basic math and counting skills. With more open competition and time to chat with friends in between turns, this fun sport is also a great social opportunity.

Chess: Strategy games are exciting and challenging at any skill level. Chess's requires critical thinking, and as a player gains skill, they can join a club and even compete in tournaments.

Painting: Painting is an activity that you can do even if you don't consider yourself artistic. You need only begin before discovering your potential for visual creativity. Even if your paintings aren't masterpieces, creating them will unlock a previously inaccessible area of your mind.

Pottery: Pottery, like painting, teaches its students a great deal about the value of practice, dedication, and thinking outside the box. Making pottery is a relaxing hobby that requires you to use your whole body. It's not about you becoming the greatest artist in the world, just enjoying yourself while stimulating your senses.

Gardening: Training yourself in the creative process of gardening allows people to develop rare abilities, even adults. Because plants are living things that enhance our lives, growing them calls for a great deal of patience and persistence. Start growing flowers on your patio or in a community garden or join a local tree-planting group. Spending time at a community garden can be just as rewarding for a budding gardener as tending to one in the comfort of one's backyard.

Importance of Non-Sport Activities and Hobbies

Overcoming boredom: Finding a form of creative self-expression helps you detox your mind and overcome boredom. Anxiety and stress can result from your everyday routine, no matter how efficiently you schedule your time. By engaging your body and mind in doing something creative, you open up yourself to experience more.

Forming relationships: Many hobbies allow you to place yourself in social settings. Even if you started alone in the comfort of your home, you could join a group to come in contact with people of like minds, which can help you build confidence and social skills.

New skills: Hobbies provide opportunities to learn and develop new skills. There is always something new to understand, whatever hobby you choose.

Time management: Pursuing a hobby is a great way to make the most of your free time. This will keep you from getting bored and will help you appreciate the value of every second. Managing time helps lead a more disciplined lifestyle and keeps you ahead in the game.

Career choices: You can only discover your hidden talents if you try something new. Hobbies can help you decide the profession you want to pursue and define your life.

Handling pressure: Life is full of ups and downs, and that includes pursuing hobbies. Sometimes you may fail, but you will learn to take these failures positively and work on your shortcomings. As you grow while pursuing your interest, not everything will go smoothly or in the perfect way you want it to, but sometimes making mistakes is the best way to learn.

Just finding joy in life: You can choose a hobby based on your passion and regularly indulge in it. Since there is no age limit for cultivating a hobby, as young adults, you know that you are choosing that hobby simply because you enjoy the activity.

CHAPTER FIVE:
SELF ESTEEM, BODY IMAGE,
AND PUBERTY

Your body is growing, your face is changing, and things have probably started looking . . . well, a little awkward. It doesn't matter if you used to be a child model, there's really no escaping the awkwardness! No doubt, you're tired of your extended family making obnoxious comments like "Oh my! Look how much you've grown!"

Let's be real — this whole "physical changes" thing is a lot to handle. It's understandable that many middle schoolers start feeling extra pressure in the looks department. Whether you're mad because that crush of yours just doesn't seem to ever be looking in your direction or you're simply confused why your nose grew before the whole rest of your face did (yeah, why?!) middle school can be a wild ride in terms of your self-confidence.

Separating the Two Siblings: Self-Esteem and Body Image

Self-esteem: Self-esteem is an internal evaluation of your value to yourself and the world. Self-esteem is a measure of confidence in your merits and abilities, much like self-respect. Motive, mental health, and quality of life all impact your self-esteem.

Body image: Your self-perception and feelings about your body make up your body image. The extent to which you are content with your physical appearance is directly related to whether or not you have a positive mental picture of yourself as you look in a mirror.

UNDERSTANDING PUBERTY AND PHYSICAL CHANGES

Depending on their background, your middle school peers may know little to nothing about puberty. However, there's no point in delaying the inevitable; in a nutshell, puberty is when a child's body starts to look more like an adult. During puberty, a child's body goes through a series of changes that prepare it to reproduce sexually as an adult. To start the process, the brain sends hormones to the gonads (the ovaries in women and the testes in men.)

These changes make you stop thinking about your relationships and feelings like a child and start thinking like an adult. How you feel physically, emotionally, and socially will change. During puberty, the body goes through some changes that happen to everyone. However, not everything happens at the same time for everyone, and it doesn't happen all at once. Because of this, it is essential to realize that a person's inner state and relationships with others can be changed just like their outward appearance.

When does puberty happen?

Most boys begin to experience puberty between 9 and 11, though it may only become noticeable at 13 or 14, just before they turn 15. Girls typically start to notice signs of puberty between the ages of 8 and 9, though some may not do so until they are 12 or 13. Don't worry if your age doesn't line up exactly, though! Each person goes through puberty at a different time, but these timelines can still be used as a general guide to how people mature physically.

The puberty processes.

In today's society, stages of development are called Tanner stages (sexual maturity ratings).

Tanner stage 1: At this point, both boys and girls go through the same changes inside. It describes what happens to you before you see any outward signs of puberty.

- The brain starts the process by sending signals to the body to prepare for changes in the form of hormones.

- The hypothalamus wakes the pituitary gland, which makes two hormones (luteinizing hormone and follicle-stimulating hormone) that control other glands in the body.

Tanner stage 2: Signifies the start of growth and development in the body. The commands are being sent all over the body by hormones.

Males

- The growth of pubic hair begins at the genital base.
- The scrotum (the area around the testicles) and the testicles start to grow in size.

Females

- During this time, the uterus enlarges, and pubic hair sprouts on the vulva lips.
- "Buds," the early stages of breast development, appear under the nipple. It's normal for one bud to be bigger than the other or for there to be some itchiness or tenderness.

- The areola, the dark ring around the nipple, will also enlarge.

Tanner stage 3: Both sexes undergo more noticeable physical changes as they progress from the previous stage.

Males

- Muscles get broader.
- As the testicles continue to enlarge, the penis also continues to lengthen.
- Breast tissue may start to develop under the nipples (it usually disappears after a couple of years).
- As the voice evolves, it may "crack," shifting from a higher to a lower pitch as it does so.
- Their height continues to rise.
- "Wet dreams," or nighttime ejaculations, are common in young adult males.

Females:

- The pubic hair becomes denser and wavier over time. Under the armpits, hair follicles begin to develop.
- The so-called breast "buds" keep growing and expanding.
- The fat deposits first appear on the hips and thighs.
- The back and face are two common locations where acne breakouts manifest.
- The rate of growth in height accelerates to its maximum potential.

Tanner stage 4: Puberty continues as males and females observe many body changes.

Males

- The hair in the armpits begins to develop.
- The voice settles into a deeper tone.
- You may start getting acne.
- The scrotum will darken in color as it continues to get larger.
- The testicles and penis will continue to grow in size.

Females

- The average annual increase in height slows to somewhere between two and three inches after this point.
- The hair in the pubic region becomes fuller.
- After passing through the bud stage, the breasts develop a fuller shape.
- It's common for girls to get their first period between 12 and 14, although it can happen earlier in some cases.

Tanner stage 5: This is the final stage of the male and female puberty journey.

Males

- The pubic hair has thickened and grown down to the inner thighs.
- Some men will have to start shaving because facial hair will begin to grow at this point.
- The growth rate in height will eventually slow down, but muscle mass might continue to expand.
- The scrotum, penis, and testicles will all have grown to their adult sizes.

- Around the age of 18, most boys have reached their full height.

Females

- Pubic hair grows to the level of the inner thighs as it thickens.
- After anywhere from six months to two years, periods become consistent.
- Females reach their full adult height one to two years after the onset of their first period.
- Even though breasts may keep evolving until age 18, they have roughly the size and shape of an adult by that time.
- All of the reproductive organs and genitals have reached their full maturity.
- The shape of the buttocks, thighs, and hips fills out.

BUILDING A POSITIVE SELF-IMAGE

Having a positive self-image and good self-esteem are extremely important to your mental health as a young teen. Many factors can influence the way you view yourself, so you need to take action to control your emotional environment as much as you can. Here are some ways you can help influence the way you see yourself in a positive way!

Leave bad friends: Get rid of people who make you feel bad and try to take advantage of you. One of the best ways to feel good about yourself is to have good relationships with people who respect and value you.

You are your own friend: When judging a friend, you are more likely to be patient, forgiving, kind, encouraging, and supportive than when judging yourself. If you're constantly being hard on yourself, take a step back, change your perspective, and talk to yourself like a friend.

Know how vital positive self-esteem is: Depression and anxiety are less likely to develop in people with a strong sense of self-worth. Realizing that how you think about yourself directly affects how happy and fulfilled you are in life can be a powerful way to start making changes for the better.

Forget others' opinions: If you're always worried about what others might think, you can't really be who you are. Stop second-guessing yourself based on what other people think and start acting in your own best interests instead of how you think other people want you to.

Create safe spaces: Setting safe and healthy boundaries can help you feel you're worth something again. Learn how to tell when someone has crossed your boundaries and how you would like to respond. Don't let people dominate you, use you, or manipulate you. To be confident, you have to set and stick to strict limits.

Love who you are: Be nice to yourself, even if there are things about you that you don't like or that you wish were different. Everyone has things they'd like to improve about themselves, so you should still think highly of yourself. People love others, but are sometimes not very good at loving themselves, even when they need it the most.

PROMOTING A
HEALTHY BODY IMAGE

Middle schoolers often start to obsess about their body image, due to the pressure they face from society to look a certain way. These societal ideas of "looking good" are sometimes very harmful, strict, and unrealistic. Because some of the newbies in school are simply trying to make new friends, they conform and think something is wrong with their bodies.

This can take a large toll on their physical and mental health. Young people have developed eating disorders, depression, and low self-esteem from trying to achieve impractical ideals.

What to Do About Body Image:

- *Repeat* "positive affirmations" to yourself. They can improve your self-esteem by helping you develop an appreciation for your self-image, making you love your body regardless of how you perceive your appearance.
- Put a cap on the amount of time you spend on social media and restrict the kinds of content you read and post.
- Be sure that you understand the changes your body is going through during puberty. Sweating, growing hair and gaining weight are natural and healthy parts of the maturation process.
- Develop good eating habits and educate yourself on how to eat a healthy and balanced diet.
- Foster the kind of beneficial friendships that are good for everyone involved. In particular, having friends who have

positive relationships with their bodies and can serve as positive role models can be beneficial.

- Taking part in various sports and other forms of physical activity, especially those not emphasizing size or shape, can help you maintain a positive image of yourself.

It is a reality that each person has a unique body type, yet you may improve your appearance by improving your diet, getting more rest, and engaging in physical activity.

DEALING WITH COMPARISONS AND MEDIA INFLUENCE

The rapid growth of social media platforms has changed how young people and the general public talk to each other today. It has become a place where people can get together to talk, learn about each other's projects, and celebrate each other's achievements. A lot happens because everyone wants to be a part of the trend.

Many things contribute to an adolescent's experience, and jumping on trends can seem important to you now. The effort to become someone else takes a lot of effort, and it's often impossible to achieve. This is especially true when likes, comments, and shares measure how popular or liked a thing is.

Dealing With the Fear of Missing Out (FOMO)

FOMO, which can result in feelings of inadequacy, is the worry that other people are enjoying themselves at social events that you are not part of. We talked about the custom of celebrating others' success, but in reality, social media may serve to embellish the truth of others' life updates.

Negative body image issues can be worsened when you compare themselves to your peers; you're already thinking a lot about how you want to present yourself to the world — probably too much, in fact. Other issues, such as anxiety, depression, lack of sleep, and low self-esteem, have all been connected to the use of social media.

Those with FOMO may feel the need to constantly monitor their social media accounts, even if doing so only makes them feel worse about themselves. As a result of not receiving "enough" feedback on their social media posts in the form of comments, likes, and shares, they may feel inadequate in the eyes of their peers.

What You Should Do:

- The first step is to learn to love yourself. Any other steps you try will not work without this initial decision. When you love yourself, it comes with the understanding that *you are unique.*
- Now, always remember social media is an amplifier; it can make something look better than it is. With filters, beauty apps, camera angles, and photoshop, you can't really trust what you see on social media platforms.
- Keep in mind that the people who have the most positive body images are those that don't compare themselves to others.

- Note that there is so much more to you than your outward appearance!
- Don't become obsessed with your phone and social media; read a book, enjoy the outdoors with friends and fill your days with other activities.
- Remember, the people who love and will love you do so because it's you, and not how you look.

CHAPTER SIX: NAVIGATING THE DIGITAL WORLD

It's a big wide digital world out there, and you're probably more than a little curious about how the heck a lot of it works and why. There's no harm there! We can guarantee you one thing—it's better to have a few of your questions answered here than have to ask your parents, right?

Let's dive into the digital world and see what sorts of things are out there. Although you probably already know a lot about this stuff, there's always more to learn and experience, not to mention, knowing how things work in "cyberspace" can help you avoid some pretty embarrassing, self-esteem-crushing situations. Now that a lot of middle schoolers have smartphones and other gadgets, the reach of things like peer pressure and bullying have extended even further than before.

Don't worry though—we'll help you make sure that totally embarrassing video of you your friends took doesn't crash your party or kill your vibe.

Key things you should know.

- The Internet and its digital world are much larger than you could imagine.
- Internet access is available to anyone, anytime, from any location, provided they have a computer, tablet, smartphone, or other device capable of connecting.
- The Internet is filled with information, but not all of it is accurate.
- If you publish something on the Internet, it will remain accessible to anyone—forever.
- The Internet can be used for many good things.

- Always keep in mind that there are bad people in the world, and they can use the Internet too.

UNDERSTANDING AND PREVENTING CYBERBULLYING

What is Cyberbullying?

Cyberbullying is when a person or group threatens or intimidates someone using the Internet and/or other electronic means of communication, like text messages. It is a vindictive and intentional behavior. An example of cyberbullying is when someone sends or posts embarrassing texts or photos about another individual without the owner's permission or knowledge.

Various Forms of Cyberbullying:

- Making someone the target of jokes on message boards is a form of group victimization.
- To cruelly and maliciously exclude someone from an online group is an example of cyberbullying.
- Spreading false information about someone to make them look bad or embarrass them is another form of cyberbullying.
- People who engage in cyberbullying may post their victims' private information (such as their names, addresses, and places of employment or education) online, a practice known as "doxxing."

- Publicly issuing threats and shaming via social media.
- Creating fake accounts, comments, or websites to defame, discredit, or ridicule a person by impersonating them.

Any form of harassment online, including impersonation, social exclusion and cyberstalking, falls under the umbrella of cyberbullying.

Anonymity in Cyberbullying

It is not uncommon for cyberbullying victims to be in the dark about who is harassing them and why. Some people who engage in cyberbullying are able to conceal their identities, making it more difficult for the perpetrator to be identified and punished for their behavior.

Preventing Cyberbullying

Bullying in the physical and digital worlds share many similarities, so it makes sense that some traditional preventive processes are used here too.

- Talk to your parents, guardians, teachers and other adults that care for you. Let your folks know what you are doing online.
- Know how the platform or app you are on works and read about it before using it.
- Avoid interacting with strangers online.
- Because of the prevalence of bullying in the digital world, most online platforms make it easy to report any form of harassment.
- Be observant and pay attention to how you interact with people online.

RESPONSIBLE SOCIAL MEDIA USE

What you post stays forever: No matter how often you delete or request that the platform remove something, it will always be accessible to the public. It's already out there on the internet when you realize you don't want it there. Remember that anything you put online will be accessible indefinitely.

Know the risks: If you're old enough for social media accounts, you should also be mature enough to handle them. To be cautious, search Google and read what various sources say about the topic.

Keep it lawful: You can learn more about what constitutes illegal content by researching. Posting illegal content — or evidence of unlawful activity — can lead to legal trouble.

Do your Research: Your web browser is the most powerful research tool at your disposal, so do your homework before committing to a social media app or platform. That way, you'll know if a brand-new platform is legit and not just trying to steal your information. Better online security only requires a little extra effort.

Nothing is anonymous: You should know that your anonymity is not what it seems online. Everyone leaves a trail of digital footprints wherever they visit online. It's as straightforward as it looks. For someone motivated, it's easy to track a person down and identify them.

Have a focus: Concentrate on just a couple of things. You can improve your concentration by using social media to augment offline activities. Read up on the topics that interest you and teach you something new. You can limit your time spent on social media by concentrating on activities that bring you joy.

Gain some value from your time online: Instead of posting an infinite number of meaningless videos, reels, selfies, gossip, or messages, be a source that gives valuable information. If you want to increase your reputation, post encouraging content that anyone can use.

Control your feed: One of your social media responsibilities is managing your feed. Don't let other people decide who you follow, or which pages you "like." Think carefully about the media you allow into your life. Learn to identify toxic accounts and remove them from your feed. If someone is being unpleasant or rude to you or others, unfollow or block them.

Share Thoughtfully and Responsibly:

- Most importantly, don't publish or spread anything construed as harassing, violent, abusive, or defamatory.
- Do not like, share, or repost content that promotes bigotry or racism.
- Only share information after first verifying its accuracy. If you share a story, even if you didn't create it, you implicitly endorse the message.
- Only share news from verified sources, and even then, make sure to fact-check the stories using tools such as snopes.com and politifact.

- Never spread untrue stories. Always check how current a story is, the bias(es) of the source or author, and the story's purpose before sharing, and never share a link to an article you haven't actually read.

INTERNET SAFETY AND PRIVACY

Cyberbullying is only one thing that could happen if you don't protect your privacy well enough. As cybercriminals come up with new ways to attack people online, their threats are always changing. There are also concerns about privacy breaches, which can lead to identity theft, malware and virus infections on your devices, phishing and scam emails sent to you, and inappropriate content.

How to Ensure Your Safety and Privacy on the Internet:

Adjust your security preferences: You can, for instance, set different permissions for different users. Who can find your digital footprint, that is, your videos, written posts and photos? These capabilities are yours to use on Facebook, Instagram, and other social media sites.

Don't try to be too friendly: Exercise caution when accepting a friend request. Verify people's identities before adding them as friends on social media; not everyone who wants to be your "friend" will treat you like one.

Protect your personal life: Avoid sharing sensitive information online, such as photos of your parents' driver's license, passport, or credit card numbers. This may seem obvious, but it's a common reason why people fall victim of scams and identity theft. You shouldn't share anything on social media that can be traced back to you personally. That includes your actual physical address, as well.

Go to trustworthy sites: Check to see if the website you intend to use has a reliable reputation, especially apps and websites where financial transactions occur. Watch for a lock icon next to the site's address in your browser to know a secure site.

Use strong passwords: Passwords that are simple to remember are often the weakest ones, making it easy for hackers to gain access. Furthermore, users are at risk if they use the same password for multiple sites, making it easy for hackers to access all sites with the same password.

Close old accounts: Don't forget about dormant accounts by failing to close them. They are vulnerable to being misused after being obtained by cybercriminals. Additionally, criminals can use the information you leave behind to access your active accounts.

Watch out for malicious files: Any app or downloadable material that looks like a game, performance booster, or a program that frees up space could be hiding malware. Inappropriate downloads can compromise your device in several ways, including altering its regular operation and stealing your personal information. Be alert and stick to downloading from reputable or official channels only.

Multi-factor authentication (MFA): MFA uses more than just a password to gain access to your online space. With MFA, users must provide not one but multiple means of verification before gaining access to their accounts online. Signing up for MFA provides an extra level of security for your personal accounts and data.

These Authenticators Include:

- Biometric data such as voice, finger or face recognition
- An additional random password that the website's authentication servers' text or email you.
- The correct answer to your secret questions.

THE PROS AND CONS OF ONLINE GAMING

Online gaming is an activity that has become a part of everyday life for some people. You'll even see people with a community of peers who've formed a social group just from gaming. The development of better technology and high-speed internet connection also makes the online gaming culture thrive and improve. Gaming is a great way to pass the time; however, it comes with issues.

The Pros of Gaming:

Develops your strategic and analytical thinking: Online games improve strategic thinking and analytical skills. Successful players think quickly and make decisions; these skills help gamers react quickly to game changes. In real life, these skills will help solve problems quickly.

It's a means of socialization: Online games can also assist shy or isolated individuals in meeting new people. Players can make international friends and even professional connections through online forums and chat rooms. Gamers who play online frequently make new friends with whom they can communicate and socialize.

You can become a better team player: Aside from socializing, online gaming allows you to collaborate to achieve a goal. People who've never even seen each other form teams and work together. For someone who's never had the chance to be part of a team, gaming with others can help them see the importance of teamwork.

It helps you relax: Gaming allows you to escape to a virtual world when real life gets to be too much, which is one reason it's become so popular over the years. Online gaming helps those suffering from anxiety and depression calm down. Adults with kids as old as you can join a gaming community, and after a difficult day, switch on their game and let the stress melt away.

It helps increase focus: Playing video games online has been shown to boost cognitive abilities and memory in young people. Completing levels of certain video games online calls for careful strategy and the ability to think outside the box. As a result, young minds learn to be more alert and focused.

The Cons of Gaming:

It opens the door for cybercriminals: There is always a chance of being hacked when playing games online. to participate, players enter personal information for a variety of reasons. That means criminals can use games to steal people's information and money.

Cyberbullying happens frequently: However, advanced the internet may become, people will always look for opportunities to exploit others. One tactic these individuals will use is cyberbullying. It's a common strategy for causing frustration among players, and the player's reputation could be destroyed within seconds.

Violence can become normalized: Even though different people may experience other effects from playing violent video games, it is still necessary to address the problem. Evidence suggests that some children who play violent video games demonstrate a similar lack of self-control and increased sensitivity.

Health concerns: Your health can be hurt by too much online gaming. Gamers spend too much time sitting still, which can cause back and shoulder pain from overuse and lack of movement. Also, research shows that every hour of play increases the risk of being overweight. Other effects include not getting enough sleep, eye problems like blurry vision, hearing loss, among other things.

Academic process could be limited: Playing games consumes a lot of time, time that could have been used for things like studying. Many gamers have been observed to put off studying or ignore deadlines to play the game they like best. Gaming can make it difficult for kids to maintain their progress in school.

Gaming becomes addictive: Some gamers get so caught up in the action that they forget to eat or shower. Not surprisingly, this is the case because persistent online gaming can lead to addiction. Players may invest a lot of time into the game, neglecting their other personal, academic, and professional commitments to focus on it. Addiction to playing video games online has become a significant issue that many people are struggling to cope with.

CHAPTER SEVEN:
BUILDING CHARACTER

"Character" is yet another buzzword you've probably heard your parents, coaches, and teachers toss around. At this point, you're probably a little tired of hearing about it, but talking about character doesn't have to be some sort of snoozefest where you're lectured about being responsible or talked down to like you're in preschool. "Building Character" is really just another way of saying "developing a healthy personality."

Everybody wants to be respected; at the very least, everybody wants to be treated like a human being. There's no way to force a "right" way of behaving on those around you, though. Your best bet for making your middle school experience a little bit more tolerable is simply to spread a little positivity and love. Although it may sound cheesy, you truly never know how big of an impact a few kind words, or a friendly smile can have.

UNDERSTANDING DIVERSITY AND INCLUSION

What's Diversity?

The range of human differences includes but is not limited to differences in physical or mental abilities and qualities, religious or ethical value systems, race, ethnicity, gender identity, sexual orientation, class, national origin, immigration status, family structure, language, and learning styles. Diversity is the wide range of differences between people.

And Inclusion?

Inclusion means that a person is part of a community, has the power to make decisions and that the community recognizes the worth and dignity of every person. A school is inclusive if it helps its students feel like they fit in and if it values and shows respect for the different abilities, beliefs, backgrounds, and ways of life of its students.

What's the Importance of Understanding Diversity and Inclusion?

It helps you and everyone else understand that despite our outward appearances, the clothes we wear, the foods we eat, and the holidays we celebrate, we are all human.

- A diverse group is more likely to have a wide range of talents and knowledge that can help them adjust to change.
- Diversity and inclusion help make everyone feel like they belong.
- By sharing your various points of view, ideas, and experiences, a diverse group can develop more creative and resourceful ways to solve problems.
- Promoting diversity helps make the world a fairer and more just place, where everyone has the same chances, and no one is denied an opportunity due to discrimination.
- You can learn about different cultures, values, and experiences by interacting with different kinds of people. This can help you develop a sense of empathy.

SHOWING RESPECT TO OTHERS

Respect is one of the best ways to achieve inclusion in middle school, and in life. Respect is an attitude or behavior that displays consideration and acceptance, regardless of differences in opinion, behavior, or belief. It expresses gratitude for admirable characteristics, and because of this, one is careful while attending to another person's wants and emotions. Respect is synonymous with regard, worth, and esteem.

To respect someone is to value what they are thinking, their time, and their privacy. If you respect someone, you consider what they have to say and act in a way that demonstrates your concern for them. You are not doing it for them, but for you. You should respect everyone whether or not you think they deserve it; everyone deserves to be treated with respect and dignity.

How to Show Respect to Others:

- To show respect, one must first consider the other person's emotions.
- Respect those who are in authority, your parents, teachers and coaches. You can respect someone even if you don't fully understand them or share their views.
- Pay attention when someone is speaking.
- Don't invade someone else's personal space. It can be upsetting and uncomfortable for them.
- Don't judge someone by what you hope they can do for you.
- Be polite.

- Maintain your self-respect, even if others do not.

EMPATHY: PUTTING YOURSELF IN SOMEONE ELSE'S SHOES

Empathy is about imagining yourself in another person's shoes and experiencing their emotions. Being empathetic means trying to see things from another person's perspective. The desire to understand another person is sparked by empathy.

How to Be Empathetic:

- Try to imagine yourself in whatever situation the other person is going through at the moment.
- Develop the skill of listening to others without inserting your opinions.
- Try letting your guard down and talking openly about how you feel.
- Get out of your comfort zone and into new experiences to better understand how others may be feeling.
- Join groups that are working to improve society.
- Focus on how people express themselves non-verbally (their body language.)
- Learn to empathize with others, even if you disagree with them.
- Inquire about people and their experiences to find out more about them.
- Improve your relationships with others to gain insight into their emotions.

- Learn more about your potential prejudices and how they may influence your ability to empathize with others.
- Try to find common ground with other people, rather than focusing on your differences.

The Importance of Empathy:

You learn personal control: Learning to control the way you react to your emotions can be aided by developing empathy for others. Learning self-control is crucial because it prevents you from letting stressful situations bring out the worst in you.

You learn to lead: Empathy will make you a better leader. Leaders need to know and connect with the people they oversee. Leadership often stresses the importance of personal growth in the role of being able to communicate with others. Anyone who aspires to become a leader should develop the capacity for empathy to connect and communicate with the people they will be guiding.

Empathy leads to helpfulness: Having empathy for others increases the likelihood that you will help those around you and the possibility that others will help you.

Better socialization: The benefits of social relationships to one's physical and mental health have been proven again and again. Having empathy makes it easier to connect with others.

Sense of community: Empathy helps students connect with peers and people outside of school by helping them understand others' feelings. Through interactions with people from other cultural backgrounds, you gain skills that will serve you well in later life.

Empathetic students bond more, which benefits the whole community of which the school is a part.

STANDING UP AGAINST BULLYING AND INJUSTICE

What's Bullying?

You've probably seen a few bullies over the years; maybe you've even been a bully yourself! We might as well go over what bullying is and how it works anyway, just to hammer some points home. Bullying is when someone "picks on," humiliates, insults, or bosses around another person. Often bullies derive a sense of power and pleasure through controlling or humiliating someone else. Sometimes bullies are individuals who've been hurt themselves and are trying to compensate for their pain, while other times they simply lack empathy. Bullying is basically everywhere, especially in middle school. Now, with the rise of cellphones and social media, bullying takes place even after school gets out.

And Injustice?

Injustice is unfairness, or the lack of justice and fairness. Injustice happens when someone's rights are being violated and not defended.

Why bullying is injustice:

When someone is picked on, it is a display of unfairness. Chances are, they might already be feeling bad about themselves. It's possible that they don't like school or feel like they're doing well there, and they are already having a hard time getting used to life here, then some flawed individuals will add to this misery by bullying them. Other students see this going on and, much of the time, do nothing to stop it.

Standing Up to Injustice:

To deal with bullies (or mean people in general), you have to be willing to stand up for yourself and others. It's not about beating people up; instead, it's about standing up for what is right and not allowing the actions of others or external circumstances to diminish your sense of worth. Your ability to handle negative emotions like anxiety, fear, depression, and confusion increases when you decide to stand up to bullies.

Thanks to your intervention, the people who care and those whose child you are defending from injustice will be overjoyed to learn that you stood up for their child and prevented them from being mistreated. You want to grow up to be a reliable source of safety for your loved ones, including your siblings, friends, and maybe even future children.

What to Do:

Don't join in: If you have joined a bully before, it becomes more difficult to stop them. People who join the bully in making fun of the victim send the message that they agree with what the bully is doing. On the other hand, people who stand up for the victim send the message that they don't like abusive behavior.

Tell an adult: Bullying often worsens if an adult doesn't do something. Talk to an older person capable of dealing with the bullies. You can talk to an adult you trust or tell a teacher or other authority figure about what happened. One way to let the right people know about the bullying—and hopefully stop it from happening again—is to file a formal complaint.

Record the incident: Mark their faces if they are too many for you to face alone. Use your phone to record their faces and go to the nearest authority and show them the video or pictures.

Firmly resist: Most bullies don't think far ahead, and don't foresee resistance. Firmly and confidently telling a bully to stop can make a big difference. Bullies often target younger kids who they think they can scare. Bullying will persist if no one speaks up, but it can be stopped if people confront bullies and make their disapproval known.

Go with friends to help you: Some people could back the bullies. To confront them with the support of your friends, you all take a stand together. If you bring your friends, and your friends come with their friends, you are more than the bullies will know how to handle.

CHAPTER EIGHT:
FAMILY RELATIONS
AND COMMUNICATION

We've mentioned family as one of the first places you should look for help. Let's face it, whether you feel that warm and fuzzy about them or not, they tend to know you better than anybody else. Hopefully they also treat you with love and respect, but, no matter what, there's no doubt that your parents have an idea what you're going through. It may sound cheesy (maybe even a little unbelievable), but your mom and dad were once stuck in that seeming toxic waste facility known as "middle school," too. They likely went through much of the same daily struggle, whether they'd like to admit it or not!

Your parents have seen a lot and probably know what you're going through. Older siblings can help, too. At the same time, younger ones will rely on your experience, so you can help them when they get to be your age. Your home protects you from problems; it becomes your shield against the outside world.

Ideally, your family is a source of joy, peace and comfort. It's also important to realize that this can be the case, even if your communication isn't always perfect and your interactions aren't always entirely pleasant. What separates a family from ordinary strangers just living together is that they try. Communication and effort reveal the family bond's strength.

When parents can express themselves to each other and pass those communication skills on to their children, the children can relate well with one another and have an atmosphere that allows them to share their feelings openly. Communicating with your parents and siblings should be natural, because they are the people who want to see you happy and successful the most.

THE ROLE OF FAMILY
IN MIDDLE SCHOOL

Your enjoyment of both middle school and life in general depend on your family's input. Some parents and siblings might see no reason to get involved in their tween's life; they might assume that since their kid is a little moody (sorry . . .) and doesn't always laugh at their jokes that they should just lay low and give up on trying to relate. However, this isn't really such a great idea. Families—and parents most especially—represent a crucial portion of children's development and wellbeing (sorry again!)

The Role of Families Includes:

- Your family can help you overcome anxiety and turn it into positive action.
- They can go over school rules and schedules with you.
- They will be your source of encouragement when you do something new, such as sports and hobbies.
- They can also be a second set of eyes. They might be able to see things you've missed.
- They're available to listen to your worries and issues and help provide and implement solutions.
- They will support you as you figure out what you believe in this new stage of life.
- They take care of you, ensuring you get healthy meals, your fees are paid, and you have the resources you need for school.
- They will ensure you get enough sleep each school night, even when you don't think you need it!

- They understand that homework gets more intense in middle school and can help you study and manage your time.
- They will help you develop responsible skills, like organization. With more homework, class activity, sports, extracurricular and interests, you'll need all the help you can get!

COMMUNICATION: SPEAKING AND LISTENING

We'll give it to you straight: the goal of this section is to encourage you to develop the habit of talking to your family members more.

What is Communication?

Communication is when you and another person share information or news with one another. It's the act of transferring knowledge, thoughts, and emotions from one location, person, or group to another.

There are many different ways of communicating with people; you can talk, text, use body language, communicate with your eyes and even use emojis. However, of all the forms of communication in the world, none is as effective as talking in person. You need to grow more comfortable talking to your parents and siblings about what happened at school and maybe even conversations you had with your friends.

So, since we are focused on this form of communication, what does it really mean? Speaking (or talking) is the act of making sounds with your mouth to express your thoughts and feelings through words. When you were a baby, before you could speak, your parents had to guess what you were feeling. They probably misinterpreted a lot; no wonder babies cry all the time!

With words, it's just easier to get problems sorted out.

How Should You Communicate with Your Family?

- Be respectful to your parents at all times.
- Be aware of your parents' availability. Don't bother them when they are on a call with their boss; wait until an appropriate moment.
- Know what you want before starting a conversation. If you are seeking advice, or you just need someone to talk to. Let them know what you need at the start of the conversation.
- Do your best to be clear about your feelings and what you want.
- Actively listen when they are speaking to you.
- Even when you disagree, don't grumble or start whining.
- Your facial expression is apparent. So don't start frowning or glaring; your parents can clearly see you, and it's disrespectful.
- Let them know how much you appreciate them and how nice it is to talk to them.

Why Communicate by Talking and Actively Listening?

Many tweens make the mistake of assuming their parents or siblings should be used to them now and know what is on their minds without speaking, but that's an unfair expectation. Your parents are busy with many things, including keeping you and your siblings happy; they may only notice things once someone points them out. It's the same with your siblings; they're figuring life out, too, and may be wrapped up in their own issues. By having good communication, everyone is heard and understood, which is what you really need from your loved ones.

DEALING WITH SIBLING RIVALRY

There will be fights, and some will be worse than others when you have a sibling (or more than one.) They're your family, but they're still different human beings. Even twins who look the same are unique individuals. This means you have to deal with several different kinds of people at home. There will be competition, and that can make people feel jealous and angry—hence, the fights.

What is Sibling Rivalry?

If it involves name-calling, constant competition for parental attention, verbal or physical fighting, tattling, bickering, and jealousy, you have sibling rivalry. It's the ongoing conflict between children brought up together in the same family. It doesn't matter whether they are related by blood or not, as long as the parents raised everyone as siblings.

Dealing with It:

Your parents can't treat you exactly the same: We already mentioned that you and your siblings have different personalities. Your parents can only get the best from you by meeting you at different levels.

Having alone time: Since they can't treat you all the same, they should, if they are not presently doing so, provide each of you with a one-on-one arrangement. It will be a chance to check in with each child alone.

Family meetings: Having meetings all together is another way to ensure everybody is heard. Your parents could introduce family meetings where everyone is seated and allowed to say what's on their mind freely, without judgment. That way, you can take steps together to address any grievances.

Respecting personal spaces: It's necessary to give your siblings their freedom when they need it. If they're in their rooms doing something important, don't bother them with something less serious. Are they having friends over? Leave them alone and do something else.

Love and respect: No matter how jealous or angry you and your siblings might get, it's crucial to remember that you all love each other. Because you love each other, mutual respect for each other should be no stranger to you guys.

UNDERSTANDING AND RESPECTING HOUSEHOLD RULES

Your parents are wiser than you because of the simple fact that they've lived longer than you; they have more experience. In addition, if you have older siblings, your parents have had practice.

Household rules: These could be simple direct instructions that your parents or guardian give you about the way of life or certain behaviors they expect from you.

Children like to test limits; it's just the way you are! Rules help you understand what behaviors are okay—and which are *not* okay. There are places where the rules can't be bent, and you'll grow up to find yourselves in those places. If you've been trained to follow rules, it won't be difficult for you to adapt.

Breaking Family Rules

Children often push the limits and break the rules to see what happens. You should understand that rules are essential, and it's understandable that there are penalties for breaking them. Keep in mind that sometimes you might forget and violate the rules you have been taught. However, consequences teach—and remind—you to be responsible.

Understanding the Rules:

Make sure you understand: This is very important; if you don't understand a rule, make sure you ask for clarification. If a rule sounds too general and you're not sure if a specific thing is included, it's okay to ask! Your parents will be happy to make sure you understand exactly what they expect from you. You can also ask why a specific rule is in place; however, keep in mind that your parents want the best for you, and you may not always be able to understand the reasons behind the rules.

Know what is expected of you: Don't do this or that; it's all well and good to be told this, but what if you don't remember? Ask your parents to write the rules down for you and display them in a place where everyone can see them. If you're not sure about something and there isn't a rule about it already, make sure you ask if it's okay, and then you can add it to the list together.

Repetition: Keep the rules fresh in your mind. Parents and children are all busy with careers and school, so it might be difficult to remember a rule that is delivered once in the family meeting. It could be pasted on the fridge or even made to look like artwork.

Know the consequences: If your parents don't tell you what the punishment is for a rule, it's okay to ask. However, as we said before, your parents know what's best for you, and as situations change, so may the consequences of breaking the rules. For instance, if you get a new gaming console, a new punishment might be added that involves removing your gaming privileges.

It must all be in love: Rules, breaking and keeping to the rules, consequences and rewards. All of these must be a result of loving each other. These rules are in place because parents love their children and want them to be equipped to face the world independently.

CHAPTER NINE: BASICS OF FINANCIAL LITERACY

As the saying goes, "*money makes the world go round*," and usually there's a lot of craziness to go along with it. There's stress associated with getting money and deciding how best to use it. Money can mean the difference between having a nice house with air conditioning and food or having a tent on the side of the highway. Chances are, you've heard your parents arguing about money at least a few times in your life (maybe even a few times *a week*.) But hey, there's got to be more to money than anxiety and your parents bickering about whether to go to Chicken Express or not . . . right?

Thankfully — there is!

In this chapter we'll talk a little about what money is, why it's so important, and what some cool ways of thinking about it are. Money doesn't have to be a hassle; in fact, if you learn a little bit about money now, you may never have to fight with your mom, dad or even your future spouse about it . . . *ever*! Wouldn't that be great?

Financial literacy: Managing money deals with somewhat stale and boring-sounding things like budgeting, investing, and handling one's credit. If you treat these things with care, though, building them like you would boost your stats on your favorite video game, you can look forward to a carefree existence — at least in terms of money!

UNDERSTANDING MONEY AND VALUE

An understanding of money and value is knowledge every person needs to have. It's crucial to have a healthy respect for money as a preteen. Convictions formed during this age remain rooted for a long time. When your parents teach you to save, they teach you to value money.

Growing up prepared relies on learning about significant aspects of life, including understanding the fundamentals of proper money management. The fact remains that as you grow older, you want better things, and these better things are more expensive than your $2 snacks. The older you get, the more expensive your life becomes—especially if you plan to attend college—which means your parents won't have as much money to buy you stuff you don't necessarily need. It may become challenging to adjust if you don't grasp the value of money and take some control of finances.

Things You Can Do to Learn About Money:

Start saving: It could be a piggy bank or a sealed container where you can slip in your savings for a while; you could even ask your parents to help you open a bank account. However, you save, keep a record of how much money you put in, or "deposit," each time, either in a book, a spreadsheet, or even an app on your phone. Even when you receive money as a gift, be responsible and save at least part of it instead of spending it all.

Pay attention to math: You will learn more advanced math in middle school; pay attention in class. You are not just learning so you can pass tests and exams; understanding math is essential to handling money. It's all numbers.

Play educational games: Don't blow hours on adventure games from which you will learn little to nothing. There are many online games geared toward middle school students that can help you master life skills like handling money.

Go with your parents to the back: Another way to prepare for the real world is to experience it firsthand. When your parents are off to the bank, go with them once in a while, or even every time. This will help you learn about the processes of financial transactions. This is also a good opportunity to open an account, and then you can do it all yourself!

Ask your parents about credit: Using credit cards requires discipline and proper tracking. You should ask a parent or guardian how to use credit, because it can be dangerous if you feel like you have more money than you do. However, that "money" isn't yours in the first place; it's basically a loan, and the bank gets extra, in the form of interest, when it's time to pay.

BASICS OF SAVING
AND SPENDING WISELY

The Art of Saving:

Have a goal: You're starting something important when you save money; the question to ask yourself is *why*? Are you saving to buy something specific? Are you saving to teach yourself to save or prevent a wasteful spending lifestyle? Perhaps you want to see your money grow. These are valuable questions to consider.

Where to place your savings: A home for your savings is important, because you want to avoid a place where you can reach and take what you have saved so easily. You might start off with a piggy bank, but when you grow more committed, there are bank accounts made specifically to encourage you to save.

Saving plan: Develop a plan for how much you want to put into savings, and how often. Are you saving a fixed amount daily or weekly? Maybe you've decided to save any time someone gives you money as a gift instead, or in addition to that. Whatever it is, take the time to plan how you want to save.

Record keeping: You could use a phone to keep track of your savings, create a spreadsheet, or do it the old-fashioned way using a book and pen—whatever works best for you. Whatever you decide, make sure you stay up to date, recording each deposit and updating your total. This way, you can keep track of how close you are to achieving your financial goals.

Be accountable to someone: Your parents or guardians are your best option, as you need someone close who will help make sure you're sticking to your savings plan. You may discover that you really didn't need someone to report to because you are serious about saving; however, it's better to have an accountability partner, even if you feel you don't need one.

Healthy Spending Habits

Learning to spend money responsibly can be difficult, but it's important. Even if you don't have anything specific in mind that you want to save for, you should practice saving; sooner or later, there will be something you want—or need—and you'll be glad you have it. However, that doesn't mean you can't spend *any* money at all. Here are some tips to help you spend your money wisely.

Differentiate your needs from wants: We touched on this briefly before. You should learn to separate your *needs* from what you simply want. Then you can arrange your budget, putting the things you *need* at the top, and the less important "wants" further down.

Understand and be in charge of your impulses: Impulses make you want to act immediately, without thinking. For example, imagine you are at the store with a friend, who wants to get a new pair of shoes; though you had no plans to buy anything, you see a pair of sneakers that you like. However, your parents just bought you sneakers a few months ago, and they're still in great shape. Buying that new pair of sneakers that you don't need right then and there would be an impulse buy, which isn't considered a good spending habit.

Avoid people-pleasing behavior: Many purchases are made less out of personal preference and more out of a desire to impress others. Consider the sneakers from the last example. They may be trendy or look cool, but are they comfortable? Would you still wear them if they weren't trendy? If you're only buying something because you think other people will be impressed, don't bother. Get something you want that will outlast a trend.

Learn to bargain and shop around: Unless you're somewhere with fixed price tags, try to negotiate a lesser price for the things you buy. Even then, you may be able to find a better price for the same thing somewhere else. Understand that most sellers will add money to the actual value of a product and trust that people won't notice. Examples of things that you may want to bargain for as an adult are insurance premiums, satellite TV, and car repairs.

THE IMPORTANCE OF EARNING

Earning money is what allows you to save in the first place. Of course, you probably won't be able to do most adult jobs as a tween; however, there are a lot of jobs you can do comfortably, even if it's just doing extra chores around the house. You need to provide something of value, either rendering a service or possessing some marketable ability, to earn money. A good work ethic will be a valuable skill that will serve you well.

Babysitting: If you know any of the parents in your neighborhood, and they trust you, you can charge a reasonable hourly rate to watch their children. A history of being a reliable babysitter says a lot about you as a responsible adult. Make flyers and have your parents give them out at local businesses or post them online to let people know you're looking for a job.

Dog walking and pet feeding services: You can earn regular income by walking or caring for pets. You might be shocked at how many pet owners need help feeding and walking their pets while at work or on vacation. Share your availability and interest with the community.

Housework: Helping people around the house or neighborhood with errands and tasks will get you some quick bucks. Making yourself available to pitch in with basic housekeeping and yard labor would connect you with more jobs. Household chores like dishwashing, laundry folding, vacuuming, weeding, lawn mowing, window cleaning, plant watering — and so many others — can all be assigned a monetary value.

Tutoring: Mentoring or tutoring other students for money, if you're good enough in one or more subjects, is a great way to make money. There are many students in middle school who need help with their academics and are willing to pay for it. To get started, you can post flyers around your school and tell your friends, too.

Sell some personal items: You can make money by selling old books, toys, clothing, furniture, shoes, watches, and more. You can sell things at a yard or garage sale or take pictures of each item and post them on online marketplaces.

Sell homemade drinks: This is a classic; find an area where people are gathered for work and set up a stand for drinks, such as lemonade. However, note the rules before setting up; it may be against the law to sell without a permit in some places.

Share talent with others: Aside from tutoring academic sessions, if you have a skill like drawing, playing music, cooking, or dancing, you may be able to teach lessons to others who want to learn. Share information about your interests and abilities with those interested in learning more and let them know you will teach for a fee.

Sell creative works: If you're artistic, or if you have access to someone who is, you can sell artwork. Let your parents help you open an account on one or several websites and ask for their help in running it.

INTRODUCTION TO BUDGETING

Budgeting is the act of prioritizing. It is the process of putting your limited financial resources toward your most essential needs. By making a budget, you can figure out your personal objectives and create a particular strategy for accomplishing them.

Why is it Important to Create a Budget?

It stops overspending: Since you have already assigned money to things that need to be paid for, you won't spend too much on something unimportant. You'll learn to ask yourself, "Where will the money come from?"

You achieve your goals: Budgets help you set and achieve targets for the future. When you can visualize achieving a goal, you'll be able to focus on spending—and saving—your money wisely.

You'll always be prepared: unexpected things happen all the time in life. The best way to prepare for an emergency is to plan for it in your budget by creating an "emergency account." Make achievable goals and start small. Before you know it, you'll have enough to handle whatever life throws at you!

Prepares you to be a responsible adult: Setting up financial security through a budget is something you won't forget. As you grow older, you'll realize a budget makes it easier to pay bills on time, save for big purchases, and handle emergencies when they inevitably occur.

CHAPTER TEN: HEALTH AND WELLNESS

Healthy: A state of being physically, mentally, intellectually, socially, and emotionally well, not just the lack of illness or disease.

Wellness: The achievement of health and happiness through personal growth. Healthy living comes from several things, such as regular physical exercise, eating well, and using spiritual and meditative practices.

Money is important, but health and wellness are the real *game-changers*. Even if you had all the money in the world, if you aren't mentally healthy or have some sort of severe injury or condition, you won't be able to enjoy that wealth!

NUTRITION FOR GROWING BODIES AND MINDS

Because the minerals, vitamins, and other nutrients your body relies on to stay healthy and function effectively cannot be delivered by eating the wrong foods or junk foods, it is essential to consume balanced meals regularly. Your body needs nutrition to stay healthy, grow, and maintain proper functioning.

Proper Nutrition:

Grains: Grains are an important source of a variety of nutrients, including dietary fiber, B vitamins, and minerals. You can find them hanging around in cereal, rice, quinoa, polenta, whole-wheat bread, oats, barley, couscous, rice, corn, oatmeal, pasta, noodles, and breakfast cereals.

Fats: Fatty foods aid in keeping your skin and hair healthy and in the development of your body. Not all fats are created equal, though. Oftentimes fats are demonized, but many fats are actually quite healthy for you. It's important to understand that some fats are more beneficial than others, like plant-based oils that are liquid at room temperature. Some sources of healthy fats include almonds, seeds, salmon, avocados, olives, and tuna. Some examples of unhealthy fats are stick margarine, butter, and lard.

Vegetables and fruits: You can never go wrong with some good ol' fruits and veggies! Your body receives vitamins, water, fiber, and antioxidants from these wonderful foodstuffs. Loading up on fruits and veggies will protect your cardiovascular system and increase your resistance to cancerous growths and stroke. Unlike other foods, it's truly difficult to have too many fruits or veggies, and unless you've stuffed your stomach so thoroughly that you can hardly stand, chances are — you can stand to have even more. The only thing you really need to monitor is your sugar intake, but the complex carbohydrates found in fruits and vegetables are loads better for you than the processed sugar used in candy and other junk foods. Despite popular belief, fruits and veggies don't have to be boring, stale or tasteless. There are tons of fun and delicious ways to eat these foods, and many fruits and veggies are quite tasty on their own.

Dairy: This group is made up of foods that have their source in milk. Dairy provides loads of calcium and protein, things you especially need during puberty to ensure you build those muscles and keep your bones nice and sturdy. Dairy products like milk, cheese, and yogurt, have nutrients your body needs. Don't overindulge, though; dairy also contains a lot of saturated fat, which can clog arteries and lead to heart disease. Luckily, you can get your calcium from foods like nuts and seeds, cereal, bony fish, tofu, and kale.

Protein-rich foods: Foods like bean sprouts, almonds, tofu, fish, eggs, beans, lentils, chickpeas, and lean meats like turkey and chicken all provide protein. During puberty, you need these protein-rich foods for growth and muscle development, since they produce higher volume of certain vitamins and minerals, such as iron, Omega-3 fatty acids, Vitamin B12 and Zinc.

How a good diet helps the mind.

Your mental and physical development can suffer when you don't pay attention to what you put in your body. A poor diet harms your entire body, including your brain; it can cause exhaustion, impair judgment, and slow reaction time. Poor diets have also been proven to be a contributing factor in the worsening of mood disorders, such as depressive and anxious disorders.

THE IMPORTANCE OF SLEEP

Almost all tweens have an irregular sleep pattern. Perhaps it's because you're entering a stage of life that needs extra energy for the body's development. Even so, it's crucial to understand that it is precisely because of puberty that the body must be allowed to rest as often as possible.

What Sleep Does for You:

Helps the heart: It restores the health and efficiency of the cardiovascular system. Your heart is doing a lot of work and needs rest to repair itself from usage.

Benefits mental health: Sleep allows the brain to reorganize itself. Getting a good night's sleep enhances various mental abilities, including memory and problem-solving skills. Getting enough sleep has additional benefits as well, including increased concentration, sound judgment, and fresh ideas.

Provides stronger immunity: If you don't sleep regularly enough, your immune system may react differently to illnesses and infections. Lack of sleep wreaks havoc on you, making fighting off even common diseases more difficult.

Reduces obesity and blood issues: Sleep lowers the risk of obesity, so it's not just about eating junk food. It also helps prevent stroke and high blood pressure.

Aids in healthy muscle growth: Deep sleep promotes the release of growth hormone. This hormone helps people of all ages build muscle and repair damaged tissue but is especially important for adolescents.

Helps sexual development: Sleep affects both sexual maturation and reproductive health. The hormones are at work here, also.

Helps the body respond optimally: The hormone insulin controls glucose levels in the blood. Getting enough sleep positively affects the body's insulin response. The risk of developing diabetes has been linked to sleep deprivation.

Better hormonal equilibrium: Maintaining a healthy balance of the hormones ghrelin and leptin, which are linked to your appetite, requires regular sleep and rest. Irregular sleep causes an increase in ghrelin and a decrease in leptin; this means you'll feel hungrier, causing you to eat more and gain weight.

DEALING WITH STRESS AND ANXIETY

Most people seem to think that preteens have nothing to worry about, but obviously, that's not the case. We are at chapter ten of this book, so it's clear that you have a lot to deal with! Without help like this, it's possible to become really overwhelmed by the thought of middle school.

- Ask yourself about what you are afraid of and write it down.
- Think about how it is causing you stress and anxiety.
- When you feel nervous, slow your breathing. Slow breathing reduces worry hormones, which calms your mind and body.
- Accept your emotions. Stress is a normal part of life.
- Speak to your parents about it. If it's about school or anything else, speak to them.
- When you speak to them, you will realize that the issue isn't as huge as it seems.
- Please don't wait for your anxiety to disappear; only when you face your fear can you get rid of it.

- Practice self-care. Self-care helps you be your best and achieve your daily goals.
- Speak positive things to yourself. You deserve to be happy.
- Have a "growth" mindset. However, always set attainable goals.
- Don't try to be perfect. Instead of always wanting things to be perfect, learn to be happy with what you put your effort into.
- Learn how to break a big assignment into manageable chunks.
- Listen to music.
- Chat with your friends, draw, write, or watch a movie.
- Eat tasty, healthy meals, enjoy them, rest and sleep.
- Make sure you're getting enough exercise.
- Be kind to people. Help out someone else. This will give you both joy and peace of mind.
- Recognize that making small changes can make you feel a lot better.

THE ROLE OF PERSONAL HYGIENE

Personal hygiene becomes important as you grow older and capable of caring for yourself. As a preteen, you need a consistent personal hygiene routine because of the onset of puberty. When you go through puberty, a lot of physical changes happen. These changes mean that you must learn different ways to care for yourself. Here are some common changes that affect both boys and girls.

- Puberty activates sebaceous glands that were previously dormant. They secrete oils rather than perspiration, which can lead to unpleasant odors, skin irritation, and other problems.
- Acne and other skin conditions are possible side effects of increased oil production and hormonal activity.
- Hair growth increases in places like the groin and armpits.
- Bad breath can be a common problem at any age.
- It's normal for girls to have vaginal discharge, even before they start menstruating.

Cleaning Yourself Up:

- Bathing is important; wash up with soap regularly, and bathe after every workout or if you get sweaty. Clean your feet, armpits, back, groin area, and bottom. After showering, apply deodorant under your arms.
- For girls, keep feminine hygiene products (such as pads and tampons) on hand, even if you aren't on your period; you never know when "Aunt Flo" will decide to make an unannounced visit.
- Pay special attention to the pubic area when showering.
- Face care involves washing your face twice daily with a gentle cleanser. Picking zits causes irritation, bacteria transmission, and permanent scars.
- Visit a dermatologist if you have acne. Although inadequate hygiene is not usually the root cause of acne, it is crucial to practice good hygiene to maintain clear skin.

- You should wash your hands before eating and after sneezing, playing with pets, or using the restroom. Keep nails clean and don't bite them.
- If you want to use perfume, body spray, or cologne, make sure you pay attention to how much you apply. There are some schools that ban these altogether because they can aggravate asthma and chemical allergies. Above all, remember this: No amount of perfume or cologne can replace showering!
- Don't share food, makeup, drinks, toothbrushes, hats, or hairbrushes. They allow the transmission of lice, bacteria, pinkeye, cold sores, and germs.
- Antiperspirant reduces sweating, and deodorant inhibits underarm odor and microorganisms. Choose one you like and use it daily.
- Don't wear anything more than once before washing. You should change socks and underwear daily.
- Hair needs vary. You should know that oily hair can make acne worse. Set a hair-washing schedule for yourself.
- Shave with a razor and shaving cream if you need to.
- Brush and floss every day. Your mouthwash can't substitute for brushing and flossing.
- Make sure the piercer is safe if you want pierced ears and let a professional do it. Learn sterilization and disposal. Clean and disinfect the new piercings.

The Role of Personal Hygiene:

- Good hygiene is essential to enjoying life to the fullest; this includes participating in activities.

- Good personal hygiene can help you avoid colds, coughs, fevers, and diarrhea. In school, when you're around many other people, cleanliness is crucial.
- Keeping yourself clean is necessary in the battle against antibiotic resistance! Practice good hygiene if you want to keep those germs away and not rely on antibiotics. It's really vital and can make a big difference.
- People will find you more attractive if you take care of yourself. It's not a secret that keeping clean will make us more appealing to other people. After all, no one wants to be around someone they can smell from across the hall!
- Having excellent hygiene can set you apart as an example for others. In light of these considerations, it is imperative that you start proper hygiene, as people tend to copy good things and respect their source.
- Good hygiene helps build confidence. Your' sense of self-worth is significantly boosted by maintaining a tidy appearance. If you take care of your essential personal hygiene—shaving, showering, and so on—you may also find it easier to approach new people.

CHAPTER ELEVEN: THE ARTS AND SELF-EXPRESSION

Even though you're not quite an adult, you've still been saddled with the whole range of human, adult emotions (we probably don't even need to remind you that, do we?) Although it can be tempting to simply "suck it up" and hide your feelings behind a smile or ignore them by binge playing Fortnite (quite tempting, we know!) it's usually a better idea to participate in a little self-expression. What do we mean when we say "self-expression," though? Well, many different things can be considered forms of self-expression, but perhaps the most common form is *art*. There are as many forms of art as there are forms of feeling, and no matter which kind of art you settle on, you're sure to be pleasantly sucked into a blissful state of mind, a state of self-expression.

Let's Understand the Two Key Terms of this Chapter:

Art: Simply put, art is human creativity in *action* and in *result*. Art encompasses a wide range of human endeavors, not only the discovery of unique talents, but skills that take years of practice.

Self-expression: Self-expression is showing what you feel, think, or want to say, especially through written or spoken word, music, visual art, or dance. It's a way to show the world who you are and how creative you can be. It also helps you learn about yourself and process your feelings.

Art is a personal and private experience that can differ for each person. Some people like art because it looks good, while others like it because it makes them feel something or think. One thing that's certain—with art, you're fully free to express yourself to your heart's content!

EXPLORING DIFFERENT ART FORMS

There are many kinds of art, some of which have only recently been developed, because new tools have been made to make them. You can try out different types of art. Here are some forms of art:

Literary arts: The literary arts focus on the written word. Activities and work related to written communication, such as writing, editing, teaching, and proofreading, are included here. All spread—speaking very generally—into three different genres: namely poetry, fiction and nonfiction.

Visual or "fine" arts: This form of art is one that relies on sight, rather than sound or text, to convey meaning. Though, historically speaking, "fine arts" included many different forms of expression—such as music and poetry—most people today use the term "fine arts" to describe any visual work that is not intended to be used for commercial or practical reasons. Painting, drawing, and sculpture are all types of visual art. The aesthetic value of fine art is independent of whatever potential utility it may have.

Applied arts: Art that serves a functional purpose is considered applied art. This form of creativity appears in many fields, including interior design, commercial signage, and architectural design. Product design and building construction are two examples of how applied art is put to practical use in the marketplace.

Performing Arts: Theater, drama, dance, music, and stand-up comedy are just a few examples of the performing arts. Performing artists are recognized for their expertise in a specific artistic discipline, though some of them tend to overlap. Ever seen a show on Broadway? That's an example of theater, dance, and music, all rolled into one! Those who engage in the performing arts include, but are not limited to, singers, actors, comedians, magicians, dancers, and musicians.

THE IMPORTANCE OF CREATIVITY AND SELF-EXPRESSION

Improved communication: Expressing yourself creatively helps you process your feelings and thoughts, which in turn helps you develop your communication skills. Communication is an essential element to society.

A better understanding of culture: Education in the arts and self-expression have broader benefits than merely academic success. They dig into human emotion, values, and experience. Since culture is the sum of human experience, including thoughts, feelings, and deeds, and understanding of different cultures helps you grow and develop your own personal culture.

An awareness of self: We have already mentioned that art involves self-expression, so this should come as no surprise. Understanding yourself entails digesting your feelings to better understand your true nature.

Better interpretation of emotions: Self-expression helps people develop many essential skills, including emotional intelligence. The creative processes of drama, painting, and music require you to draw on your experiences and explore your emotions.

Creative thinking: Creativity encourages people to develop their imaginations and exposes them to new ways of expressing themselves.

Encourages perseverance: The arts inspire a willingness to persist, because you want to achieve mastery of a skill or discipline. This drive to succeed can be applied to achieving academic success and realizing personal and professional goals throughout middle school—and beyond.

Appreciation of constructive criticism: To improve, you must both apply and receive judgment. Artists must learn to appreciate constructive criticism of their creativity and expressiveness. It can be hard not to become discouraged in the face of criticism and not quit because of it, but learning to use feedback as motivation to improve will help you in future.

Exercising the brain: Self-expression—through music, for example—improves memory, literacy, executive functioning, and foreign language proficiency. Creativity may attract tweens to a diverse, refined undertaking that mixes science, language, history, and mathematics with culture.

Simplification of other subjects: The arts are a great way to connect all of your school's topics. They also deliver concepts well. For example, a singer will often need to sing in foreign languages and interpret different rhythms and time signatures using fractions.

Increased confidence: Even the most nervous person can flourish by participating in artistic pursuits and being encouraged by teachers, club members and friends.

Development of a future mindset: Schools serve all students by training them for creative and self-expressing professions and giving them the knowledge and skills they need to succeed in college.

Planting a growth mindset: Students must balance the innate and external drive to grow. We initially learn something new because we enjoy it (innate motivation). This enthusiasm will motivate us to keep learning and growing in all areas of life.

BALANCING ARTS AND ACADEMICS

Participating in hobbies outside school can relieve stress and improve your mental health. Taking breaks from hard academic work to do things you enjoy can help you feel less stressed, stay more focused, and do better in school overall.

Tips on maintaining the right balance.

- Schedule your meals and sleep.
- Study in the morning and prioritize academics.
- List all your daily tasks and create a timetable that fits your routine.
- To stay awake and healthy, eat a balanced diet regularly.

- Smartphones and post-it notes can serve as reminders to maintain schedules.
- Encouragement will keep you interested in academics and art.
- Choose extracurricular activities based on your interests, not others'.
- Try something short-term if you're unsure about long-term participation.
- Be consistent in routine, praise, encouragement, and self-discipline. Attitude makes life more meaningful. A balanced life requires both academics and creative self-expression.
- Friends can help you through challenging times and keep you motivated in your work.
- Always communicate with parents, friends, teachers, and instructors.

ART AS A MEANS OF COMMUNICATION AND THERAPY

When you first start going to school, you most likely haven't learned how to express your emotions in a healthy and appropriate way. Young kids often release floods of tears, shout with happiness, or scream and throw a fit when they don't get their way. As you grow older, it's important to learn to communicate your thoughts and feelings in ways that are productive, rather disruptive and harmful.

Importance of Communicating Your Feelings

The capacity for self-expression is not only innate to the human species. It's been shown that stopping an emotion from fully expressing itself makes the brain networks that control that emotion slow down; this is because our emotions must be allowed to be what they need to be. If you just shove your feelings in a corner and ignore them, in a short amount of time, they will clog up everything, and the essential "feel-good" chemicals that control our behavior will be unable to flow freely.

Using Art to Communicate and as a Means of Therapy

There are times when you need to do more than just say what you are going through. Expressing ourselves creatively lets us share how we feel and wakes us up, getting our artistic juices flowing. If you are ready to take part in the process, it doesn't take much work to feel emotions right away through art. This can be done through any form of art that lets you show your deepest thoughts and feelings, like drawing, painting, sculpting, music, dance, writing, or playing.

You can still participate even if you aren't "good" at these things. They're just a way for you to say something about yourself. When you make a piece of art, you find new ways to express yourself and show other people your new ideas. Who knows? You might even inspire someone else!

CHAPTER TWELVE: PREPARING FOR YOUR FUTURE

EXPLORING INTERESTS AND PASSIONS

Middle school comes with tons of ways to discover brand new passions and interests. For example, you can:

Join an extracurricular activity: Clubs are fantastic for making friends, learning new skills, and discovering new interests. Art, music, outdoor activities, cuisine, athletics, STEM (Science, technology, engineering, and mathematics), and dance are just several examples of activities you might find clubs for. You can even start your own if you can't find one you like!

Play sports: Organized sports can help you hone your social skills, make new friends, and improve your self-confidence. Playing sports also comes with loads of physical and mental health benefits.

Get involved in the outdoors: Go outside, especially if you can get out with your family. Don't waste these awesome opportunities, especially if you live in a nature-infused area; go camping, fishing, or hiking; if you don't have access to somewhere you can participate in these kinds of activities, gardening is a great way to get outside in the sunshine. Nature has a way of seeding some pretty incredible and creative ideas, and sunlight makes your body produce vitamin D, which helps your body absorb calcium to produce healthy bones.

Walk with passionate students: Don't leave your friends behind if they haven't found their passions or interests. However, you can make friends with people who have an interest they are pursuing too; you can never have too many friends if they're helping you grow. People with passion inspire others to find their own special interests!

Be curious: Remember how when you were younger, as a toddler or infant, you were somehow curious about everything under the sun? We were all insatiably curious at that age, and that was a pretty incredible thing. Try to recapture that feeling by looking at things with fresh eyes; you never know what you might find!

Let passion-driven success stories inspire you: To stay motivated and progress as a student, you can always tap into some inspiration from a few master teachers and thinkers. There are hundreds of thousands of videos on the internet about all sorts of different passions and interests. Listen to TED Talks, read education blogs, and use social media to learn more about what you like and discover new topics to dive into.

Middle school electives: Electives can supplement your learning and introduce you to new topics. These new subjects can help you find new passions to explore in high school and beyond. Health and wellness, leadership, history, artistic exploration, reading, cooking, life skills, creative writing, and performing arts are examples of middle school electives you can dive into.

CAREER EXPLORATION: BROADENING YOUR HORIZONS

Once you know more about your beliefs, abilities, interests and character, you can start looking into possible careers (admittedly kinda boring, we know . . . but it's not gonna go away, so we've gotta stick with the program here.) "Career exploration" is a fancy name for browsing through various jobs that might spark your interest or inspire you in one way or another. As you look into different jobs, you'll no doubt find that some fit your interests better, whereas others promise a more secure and stable (ahem: *boring*) career path. As with most things in life, it's best to seek some sort of balance, ideally something that is both inspiring *and* secure. For many people, this is a lifelong journey, so why not get a jumpstart and find that passion of yours? It may just become the best job ever!

How to Explore Careers While in School:

ABC careers activity: Create occupations and abilities for each letter of the alphabet. Mark your skills and how they could be significant for each one. You could also list skills you think you'll need for a profession.

Speak to adults: Talk with your teacher or counselor to help with your exploration and plan. They'll either already know the abilities you need to qualify, or they can help you find out; they can also help you along with the educational requirements and coursework you'll need for your chosen field.

Go to a job fair: Talk to employers and ask about different jobs at a job or career fair. Job fairs are a great opportunity for you to practice interview skills. If your school doesn't have a job fair, you can always visit one nearby.

Take the basics seriously: Consider your hobbies, likes, and motivations. You can take a deeper look into those projects, topics and subjects you particularly enjoyed, and see what careers use them.

Participate in role-play employment interviews: This game lets you explore new jobs while having fun. Answer generic questions to help you connect your talents, qualities, shortcomings, and background to occupations.

Go online: This stage provides further information about jobs that fit you. Take a free online job survey to find careers that match your interests, abilities, and background; you can also study job descriptions, average earnings, career outlook, necessary education and training, and everyday tasks.

Try to learn from experts: Your teacher can help you look for work shadowing opportunities in careers that interest or suit you. Job shadowing lets students experience different jobs firsthand.

THE ROLE OF EDUCATION IN YOUR FUTURE

Education is one of the most critical factors in determining your future, and it does so in the following ways:

- It equips you with the knowledge and skills you need to successfully navigate the world and make decisions based on accurate information.
- It provides the needed support for your endeavors to grow in many ways, including emotionally, physically and socially.
- Education makes it easier to connect with others in and around your community. You won't believe how awesome life can be when you have healthy and meaningful relationships with other people.
- Participation in educational programs helps develop problem-solving, communication, and critical-thinking abilities, without which success would be impossible.
- You are prepared to adapt to technological changes in the employment market and the world; many companies use unique forms of technology, whether it's software or hardware, and the more quickly and efficiently you can learn to use these, the better.

In light of these and other (admittedly rather formal and dry sounding) benefits of education, you should have no doubt that after you graduate as an eager and motivated student, you'll be set for success. As you progress through the different levels of your education, the most important thing you should take away — aside from the knowledge you need to operate in society — is the ability to think critically and independently. That's the goal of any form of education. If you've forgotten everything else, the most important thing is that you can think and reason for yourself.

DEVELOPING LIFE SKILLS

Respect, self-advocacy, time management, collaboration, compassion, logical thinking, problem solving, and communication are just a few life skills that middle school students are on a fast track to acquire. In middle school, you may often feel uncertain as you navigate shifting relationships, groups, and incorrect assumptions about recognition, academic success, and identifying true friends. In these ways, middle school is the perfect place to test out and develop the whole toolbox of life's most essential skills.

Compassion: The most effective way is to show compassion daily is by helping, being kind and genuine, complimenting people, and showing interest by asking about their day or weekend.

Time management: In middle school, you'll have to begin to manage your academic schedule and homework. This requires you to develop time management and organization skills. Middle school demands greater organization to combine studies, extracurricular activities, and socializing. Learn to use calendars, organizers, and digital tools to assist you in time management, which will aid you in high school and beyond.

Collaboration: As a middle schooler, there are several ways to learn collaboration—practicing group work and activities is perhaps the best way. Joining a school club or team can help you learn how to collaborate as well. Collaborating with peers on group projects and attentively listening to them is another way to learn teamwork.

Conflict resolution: If you only settle disputes with fistfights, you will be in a world of hurt (literally and figuratively!) Both middle school and high school are perfect environments in which to learn conflict mediation and resolution skills. Clear and direct communication is the key that unlocks nearly every aggressive door.

Respect: You can show respect by being kind and following your parents' and teachers' rules. Observing people and how they treat others can also teach respect.

CONCLUSION:

Many people say middle school was the best time of their lives, and nothing is stopping you from saying that very same thing one day. It's often been said that *knowledge is power,* and, at the very least, knowing a bit more now than you did about what this whole middle school thing is all about gives you a little more power.

In *Middle School Survival Guide,* you learned about the changes your body is undergoing (sorry, we have to mention that again!) We also touched on how even though everybody goes through puberty, it can look different for each person (yikes again . . . we know). In *Middle School Survival Guide,* you also learned how dangerous the internet can be, even though it's also incredibly awesome and a great tool for research. You also picked up a little bit of social wisdom, some tips and tricks on how to deal with all sorts of folks, from punks and bullies to teachers, parents and friends. You were thrown a little bit of academic wisdom, some tips and tricks on how to seize your academic life by the backpack and never look back. We also tossed you a little bit of emotional wisdom, how to treat yourself right and motivate yourself in a healthy way.

All in all, it's been a wild and thoroughly enjoyable journey for us, and we hope you'll at least halfway agree!

Made in United States
North Haven, CT
08 April 2024

51046248R10080